2023

GREEN MEDITERRANEAN DIET COOKBOOK

By Cook Delicious Press

A BOOK FOR
PRESS

Green Mediterranean Diet Cookbook
How to Get Started to Live Healthier, Eating Well Every Day with Easy and Delicious Recipes On The Budget & a 28-Day-Stress-Free Meal Plan for Losing Weight. Bonus Meal Planner for Beginners included

was published by A Book For press

www.abookforpress.com

info@abookforpress.com

Sign up for **FREE BOOKS** at
our **email list**

abookforpress.com/free-books/

and join the Facebook group
for **free and new books**

@abookforpress

A Special Request

Your brief Amazon review could really help us.
I'd love to hear your honest opinion,
even with photo or video of the book,
here or scanning the code:

https://abookforpress.com/reviewus

Thank you!

Table of contents

Cooking Measurement Chart

WEIGHT		MEASUREMENT				TEMPERATURE	
IMPERIAL	METRIC	CUP	ONCES	MILLIMETERS	TABLESPOONS	FARENHEIT	CELSIUS
½ oz	15 g	2 cup	16 oz	480 ml	32	150 °F	65 °C
1 oz	29 g	1 cup	8 oz	240 ml	16	200 °F	93 °C
2 oz	57 g	¾ cup	6 oz	177 ml	12	250 °F	121 °C
3 oz	85 g	2/3 cup	5 oz	158 ml	11	300 °F	150 °C
4 oz	113 g	½ cup	4 oz	118 ml	8	350 °F	180 °C
5 oz	141 g	3/8 cup	3 oz	90 ml	6	400 °F	200 °C

What is Mediterranean Diet

The Mediterranean diet is one of the healthiest diets in the world. Based on the whole, unprocessed foods that are high in antioxidants, healthy fats, and fiber, this cookbook has tons of delicious recipes that will help you get started on your own green Mediterranean diet journey!

The Mediterranean Diet is a way of eating inspired by the traditional cuisine of countries bordering the Mediterranean Sea. The diet is rich in plant-based foods like fruits, vegetables, legumes, whole grains, and healthy fats like olive oil and nuts. It also includes moderate fish and poultry and very little red meat.

What makes the Mediterranean Diet so healthy?

For starters, it's rich in antioxidants and healthy fats, which help protect against chronic illnesses like heart disease and cancer. It also benefits blood sugar levels, cholesterol levels, and weight management. Additionally, it emphasizes eating fresh fruits and vegetables, whole grains, and legumes, which are excellent sources of fiber that can help keep you full longer.

The Mediterranean Diet also encourages a moderate intake of alcohol, typically in the form of red wine. Studies have found that this type of drinking may reduce the risk of certain types of cancer, heart disease, and stroke. Lastly, it focuses on enjoying meals with family and friends. This is an important part of the Mediterranean lifestyle, as it helps to promote a sense of community and relaxation.

The Mediterranean Diet is a great choice for anyone looking to improve their health and well-being. With delicious recipes, healthy fats, and fiber, plus the added potential benefits of red wine, this diet can help you lead a healthier life. Try adding some Mediterranean-inspired meals to your weekly menu, and you'll be on your way to a healthier lifestyle.

What is the new Green Mediterranean Diet

The traditional Mediterranean diet is considered one of the healthiest in the world. But a new, greener version of the diet is emerging, even healthier than the original. The new Green Mediterranean diet is based on the same healthy principles as the original but with an added emphasis on plant-based foods.

The diet is rich in fruits, vegetables, whole grains, beans and lentils, nuts and seeds, fish, and healthy fats like olive oil. It's been linked to lower rates of heart disease, cancer, and other chronic diseases. And unlike many other diets, the Mediterranean diet is sustainable and easy to follow long-term.

The new green Mediterranean diet also focuses on seasonal and local foods, sustainable seafood, organic produce, and whole grains. It encourages you to eat fewer processed foods and red meat while focusing instead on plant-based proteins like legumes, nuts, and seeds. Eating more plant-based meals is a great way to reduce your carbon footprint and help protect the environment.

The Mediterranean diet is also rich in antioxidants and polyphenols, which support the immune system and help protect against disease. And because it's naturally low in saturated fat, it can help reduce cholesterol levels. Finally, because it focuses on real food rather than processed or refined products, you won't have to worry about hidden fats or sugars.

In summary, the new green Mediterranean diet is a great way to enjoy delicious and nourishing meals while promoting your health and protecting the environment. It's an easy-to-follow, sustainable approach that can help you maintain your health for years to come!

How does it works exactly

The Green Mediterranean diet is a type of diet that is based on the traditional eating habits of people who live around the Mediterranean Sea. They eat plenty of fruits, vegetables, whole grains, nuts and beans, and olive oil. They also enjoy moderate amounts of fish and poultry and drink red wine in moderation.

So what are the benefits of following this type of diet?

There are many different ways that it can improve your health. For starters, the high amount of fruits and vegetables provides you with antioxidants, which help to protect your cells from damage. Whole grains are a good source of fiber, which can help to reduce your risk for heart disease and other chronic conditions such as obesity and diabetes. The nuts and beans provide protein and healthy fats, while the olive oil helps to lower bad cholesterol levels and reduces your risk for heart disease. And finally, moderate alcohol intake from drinking red wine may help to protect against stroke and dementia.

Are exercises important on the Green Mediterranean Diet?

The Green Mediterranean Diet is a healthy diet that has recently gained popularity. The main focus of this diet is to eat fresh, unprocessed foods that are locally sourced. While there are many benefits to following this type of diet, one of the most important is the importance of exercise. Exercise is essential to staying healthy and maintaining a good weight while following the Green Mediterranean Diet.

The Importance of Exercise

Regarding being healthy, exercise is just as important as what you eat. It might even be more important. When following the Green Mediterranean Diet, it is important to focus on physical activity as much as possible. This could include walking, running, cycling, swimming, or even playing a sport. Regular exercise will help you stay in shape and keep your body healthy. It also helps reduce stress and improve mood.

The Benefits of Exercise

Exercising can help reduce your risk of heart disease, stroke, high blood pressure, and type 2 diabetes. Exercise also boosts your energy levels throughout the day and can help improve sleep quality. Additionally, it helps strengthen muscles and bones and can help you maintain a healthy weight. All these factors are important for anyone trying to follow the Green Mediterranean Diet.

Tips for Exercising On the Green Mediterranean Diet

Suppose you are following the Green Mediterranean Diet. In that case, it is important to make sure that you include exercise in your routine. Try to incorporate some physical activity into each day and aim for at least 30 minutes daily. Some activities that you could do are running, swimming, cycling, or walking. If you want to increase the intensity of your workout, try HIIT (High-Intensity Interval Training), strength training, and yoga.

In conclusion, exercise is essential to following the Green Mediterranean Diet. Regular physical activity can help reduce your risk for numerous chronic diseases and can help you maintain a healthy weight. Make sure to incorporate some exercise into your daily routine for the best results.

Pros and cons of the Green Mediterranean Diet

The Green Mediterranean diet is an adaptation of the traditional Mediterranean diet that emphasizes the consumption of plant-based foods, such as fruits, vegetables, whole grains, beans, and legumes, as well as healthy sources of fat like olive oil and nuts. It has been linked to numerous health benefits, including a reduced risk of heart disease, diabetes, and some types of cancer.

The main advantage of the Green Mediterranean diet is its focus on nutrition from plant-based foods, which are high in essential nutrients such as vitamins, minerals, antioxidants, and fiber. These foods provide various health benefits that can help reduce inflammation, improve digestion and increase energy levels. Additionally, since the Green Mediterranean diet encourages the consumption of healthy fats like olive oil, it can help reduce cholesterol levels and improve heart health.

One of the potential drawbacks of the Green Mediterranean diet is its restrictions on meat and dairy products. While these foods can be incorporated into the diet in moderation, it does limit your intake of essential nutrients found in these food groups. Additionally, the diet can be challenging to follow due to its emphasis on fresh, unprocessed foods, which can be more expensive and time-consuming.

Although the Green Mediterranean diet has its benefits and drawbacks, research suggests it is a healthier option than most other diets. It encourages eating nutritious plant-based foods while allowing for some animal products in moderation. By following the principles of this diet, you can enjoy various health benefits that will help keep you healthy and fit.

How to start a Green Mediterranean Diet?

The benefits of following a Green Mediterranean diet are many. You will lose weight, have more energy, and reduce your risk for heart disease, cancer, and other diseases. Here are some tips on how to start a Green Mediterranean diet: -

- Eat plenty of fruits and vegetables every day: Include various colors in your meals to get all the necessary nutrients.

- Eat whole grains instead of processed foods: Whole grains are high in fiber and nutrients, and they will help you feel full longer.

- Include healthy fats in your diet, such as olive oil and avocados: Healthy fats help keep your body healthy and can even reduce your risk for heart disease.

- Drink red wine in moderation: Red wine has antioxidants that can protect your heart health.

- Get regular exercise. Exercise helps improve your overall health and can even help you maintain a healthy weight.

- Reduce or eliminate processed foods and sugary snacks from your diet: These foods can increase your risk for health problems like obesity and type 2 diabetes.

- Get enough sleep each night: Sleep helps keep your body and mind balanced, which is important for overall health.

Following a Green Mediterranean diet can bring many health benefits. Not only will you lose weight and have more energy, but it can also help reduce your risk for certain diseases. Start today and make small changes to your diet to improve long-term health.

Contact your doctor or dietician for more information and helpful tips on following a Green Mediterranean diet. They can help you develop an individualized plan that is right for you!

Following a Green, the Mediterranean diet can be easy and rewarding with the right steps. You will soon find yourself feeling healthier, stronger, and more energized. So, what are you waiting for? Start today and make the most of your health!

The food list to follow

Food to eat

There are endless possibilities when creating meals based on these guidelines. Here are a few examples:

- Omelet with spinach, tomatoes, and feta cheese

- Salad with mixed greens, roasted peppers, diced cucumber, olives, and feta cheese

- Roasted salmon with lemon garlic sauce

- Black bean burger with avocado mayo

- Zucchini noodles with Parmesan cheese and tomatoes

- Greek salad of cucumbers, tomatoes, feta cheese, olives, and red onion

- Grilled fish tacos with avocado salsa

- Whole wheat pasta primavera with vegetables

- Quinoa bowl with roasted vegetables, feta cheese, and a lemon vinaigrette

- Roasted eggplant stuffed with spinach, feta cheese, and pine nuts

These are just a few examples of how to use the Mediterranean diet food list. There are hundreds of recipes that can be tailored to fit the guidelines. With so many delicious and healthy options, making the Mediterranean diet a part of your lifestyle is easy. So go ahead and give it a try! You won't regret it. By following the Mediterranean diet, you can enjoy delicious and nutritious meals that will help you maintain a healthy lifestyle. It's easy to improve your health and reduce your disease risk. Plus, you'll enjoy a wide variety of flavorful and colorful dishes. So, what are you waiting for? Give it a try today!

While following the Mediterranean diet food list, include plenty of fresh fruits and vegetables. Try to buy seasonal produce whenever possible, as it is usually more flavorful and nutritious than frozen or canned. Also, keep portions in check and include physical activity as part of your daily routine to ensure you get the most health benefits.

With some planning and tasty recipes, the Mediterranean diet can easily become part of your everyday life. Enjoy!

Food to Avoid

- Junk food is any food that is high in calories but low in nutrition. It includes processed foods, fast foods, and artificial sweeteners. These food types are bad for you because they are loaded with unhealthy fats, sugars, and chemicals. Eating too much of these types of food can increase your risk for obesity, diabetes, heart disease, and other chronic illnesses.

- Processed foods are usually not as healthy as fresh ones and often contain additives. They can be high in sodium, sugar, fats, and calories but low in essential vitamins, minerals, and fiber. These types of food can also be difficult to digest and provide little nutrition.

- Fast foods are typically high in calories, saturated fat, and sodium. Eating too much fast food can cause weight gain, high blood pressure, and other health problems.

- Artificial sweeteners such as aspartame can increase your risk of cancer, diabetes, and heart disease. They can also cause headaches and other unpleasant side effects.

Avoiding these types of food when trying to follow a Green Mediterranean diet is important. Instead, focus on eating healthy whole foods naturally rich in vitamins, minerals, and fiber. This includes fresh fruits and vegetables, lean proteins such as fish or chicken, nuts and seeds, legumes, beans and lentils, whole grains such as quinoa or brown rice, low-fat dairy products like yogurt or milk, and healthy fats from avocados or olive oil. Eating these types of food will help you get all the nutrition you need while sticking to a healthier lifestyle.

In addition to avoiding unhealthy foods, it is important to limit the consumption of alcohol and caffeine. Too much of either can lead to health problems such as dehydration, insomnia, and anxiety.

Avoiding processed sugars and eating smaller meals throughout the day can help you maintain a healthy weight. Eating a balanced diet that includes all these foods will ensure you get all the nutrients your body needs while following the Green Mediterranean diet.

By following this food list, you can be sure that you are making healthy choices for yourself and your family. Eating various fresh fruits and vegetables, lean proteins, whole grains, low-fat dairy, and healthy fats is essential for optimum health. Avoiding processed foods, fast foods, artificial sweeteners, and excessive alcohol and caffeine are also important for a healthy diet. With these tips in mind, you can easily follow a Green Mediterranean diet that will provide you with all the nutrition your body needs.

What are the potential short and long term benefits of the green Mediterranean Diet

The green Mediterranean diet is an increasingly popular way of eating that emphasizes whole, unprocessed plant-based foods such as fruits, vegetables, legumes, nuts, seeds and whole grains. This type of eating has many potential benefits for both short-term and long-term health.

In the short term, one of the most notable benefits is weight loss. The green Mediterranean diet focuses on lean proteins such as fish or poultry as well as plenty of fresh fruits and vegetables. Eating a variety of these types of foods can help you feel fuller for longer and reduce your overall calorie intake which can lead to weight loss. In addition to promoting weight loss, the green Mediterranean diet has been shown to have numerous other health benefits including improved cardiovascular health and better blood sugar control.

In the long term, some studies have found that following a green Mediterranean diet may reduce the risk of certain chronic diseases such as diabetes, heart disease and cancer. This type of eating also supports brain health by providing essential vitamins and minerals that are beneficial for cognitive function. Furthermore, it has been shown to boost mood because of its emphasis on healthy fats such as olive oil which can reduce inflammation in the body.

Overall, the green Mediterranean diet is an incredibly beneficial way of eating that offers many potential health benefits both in the short term and long term. This type of eating encourages the consumption of plenty of fresh fruits and vegetables as well as lean proteins like fish or poultry which provides essential vitamins and minerals for overall good health. In addition to aiding in weight loss and improved cardiovascular health, this type of diet can also reduce inflammation in the body which can lead to better mental clarity and improved moods.

The cookbook

Breakfast

Greek Eggs

Prep Time: 10 mins

Cook Time: 5 mins

Servings: 2

Ingredients

- 1 tbsp butter

- 3 eggs

- 1 tsp water

- ½ cup crumbled feta cheese

- Salt and pepper to taste

Directions

Heat butter in a skillet over medium-high heat. Beat eggs and water together, then pour into pan. Add feta cheese, and cook, stirring occasionally to scramble. Season with salt and pepper.

Breakfast Egg salad

Prep Time: 10 min

Cook Time: 45 min

Servings: 4

Ingredients

- 8 eggs

- 2 tbsp (30 mL) mayonnaise

- 1 tbsp (15 mL) finely chopped fresh chives

- 2 tsp (10 mL) Dijon mustard

- ¼ tsp (1.25 mL)each salt and pepper

- 4 English muffins, split and toasted

- 1 cup (250 mL) shredded mild Cheddar cheese

Directions

- Place eggs in bottom of large saucepan in single layer; pour in enough cold water to cover eggs by at least 1 inch (2.5 cm). Bring to boil over high heat; cover and remove from heat. Let stand for 12 minutes; drain and rinse under cold water. Peel eggs and chop. Let cool completely.

- Combine eggs, mayonnaise, chives, mustard, salt and pepper. Spoon egg salad onto each English muffin half. Top evenly with cheese. Broil for about 2 minutes or until cheese starts to melt.

Date Oats

Prep Time: 2 mins

Cook Time: 5 mins

Servings: 1

Ingredients

- 1 large cup water

- A pinch cardamom

- A pinch cinnamon

- A pinch salt

- 3 heaped tbsp instant oats

- 2 tbsp milk

- 6 dates chopped

- 1 tbsp honey increase for sweetness

Directions

- Mix in the ingredients from water to oats in a small saucepan, and bring to boil. Once the oats start thickening, add in the milk and just allow to heat. Switch off the flame, add in the dates and the honey.

- Dig in to a healthy breakfast!!!

Italian Frittata

Prep Time: 25 mins

Cook Time: 25 mins

Servings: 6

Ingredients

- ½ cup diced salami

- ½ cup artichoke hearts, drained and chopped

- ½ cups chopped cherry tomatoes

- 1 (4.5 ounce, 127 grams, 0,28 pound) can sliced mushrooms, drained

- 6 eggs

- ⅓ Cup milk

- 2 green onions, chopped

- 1 clove garlic, minced

- 1 tsp dried basil

- 1 tsp onion powder

- 1 tsp salt

- Ground black pepper to taste

- ⅓ Cup grated Parmesan cheese

- 1 cup shredded mozzarella cheese

Directions

- Preheat oven to 425 degrees F (220 degrees C). Grease a shallow 2-quart baking dish.

- Heat a skillet over medium heat; cook and stir salami, artichokes, tomatoes, and mushrooms until heated through, about 4 minutes. Transfer salami mixture to baking dish.

- Whisk eggs, milk, green onions, garlic, basil, onion powder, salt, and black pepper in a large bowl; pour eggs over salami mixture. Sprinkle with mozzarella cheese and Parmesan cheese.

- Bake until eggs are set and cheese is melted, about 20 minutes.

Toast with avocado

Prep Time: 3 mins

Cook Time: 2 mins

Servings: 3

Ingredients

- 3 slice of bread

- 1 ½ ripe avocado

- Pinch of salt

Directions

- Toast your slice of bread until golden and firm.

- Remove the pit from your avocado. Use a big spoon to scoop out the flesh. Put it in a bowl and mash it up with a fork until it's as smooth as you like it. Mix in a pinch of salt (about ⅛ teaspoon) and add more to taste, if desired.

- Spread avocado on top of your toast. Enjoy as-is or top with any extras offered in this post (I highly recommend a light sprinkle of flaky sea salt, if you have it).

Oatmeal with bananas and almonds

Prep Time: 5 mins

Cook Time: 10 mins

Servings: 1

Ingredients

- 1 small banana

- 1 cup almond milk

- 1 tbsp honey

- 1 tsp almond extract

- ¼ tsp ground cinnamon, or more to taste

- 1 pinch salt

- ½ cup rolled oats

Directions

- Mash half the banana in a saucepan. Whisk almond milk, honey, almond extract, cinnamon, and salt with the mashed banana until smooth; bring to a boil and stir oats into the mixture. Reduce heat to medium-low and cook at a simmer until the oats are tender and the moisture has been absorbed to your desired consistency, 5 to 7 minutes. Transfer oatmeal to a bowl.

- Dice remaining banana half. Top oatmeal with banana and more cinnamon, as desired.

Yoghurt and berries

Prep time: 5 mins

Servings: 1

Ingredients

- 1 cup nonfat plain Greek yogurt

- ¼ cup blueberries

Directions

- Place yogurt in a bowl and top with blueberries.

Tomato and prosciutto sandwiches

Ingredients

- 8 (1-ounce, 28 grams, 0,06 pound) slices 100% whole-grain bread

- ¼ cup canola mayonnaise

- 2 tablespoons chopped fresh basil

- 1 teaspoon Dijon mustard

- 1 small garlic clove, minced

- 1 cup baby romaine lettuce leaves

- 8 (1/4-inch-thick) slices tomato

- 3 ounces (85 grams, 0,18 pound) very thin slices prosciutto

Directions

- Preheat broiler.

- Arrange bread slices in a single layer on a baking sheet. Broil bread 2 minutes on each side or until toasted.

- Combine mayonnaise, basil, mustard, and garlic; spread mayonnaise mixture evenly over 4 bread slices. Layer 1/4 cup lettuce and 2 tomato slices over each serving; top evenly with prosciutto and remaining bread.

- Fruit salad: Combine 1 teaspoon fresh lime rind, 1 tablespoon fresh lime juice, 1 tablespoon honey, and a dash of salt; drizzle over 4 cups mixed precut fruit.

Artichoke and cucumber hoagies

Prep Time: 10 minutes

Cook Time: 0 minutes

Servings: 4 hoagies

Ingredients

- 4 hoagie rolls

- 1 can artichoke hearts, drained and sliced

- 1 cucumber, thinly sliced

- 4 slices provolone cheese

- 1/2 cup mayonnaise

- 1/4 cup diced red onion

- 2 tablespoons diced pickled jalapeños

- 2 tablespoons diced sun-dried tomatoes

- Salt and pepper to taste

Directions

- Preheat the oven to 350°F.

- Slice the hoagie rolls in half lengthwise and place them on a baking sheet.

- Top the bottom half of each roll with a slice of provolone cheese.

- In a small bowl, mix together the mayonnaise, red onion, jalapeños, and sun-dried tomatoes. Spread a generous amount of the mayo mixture on the top half of each roll.

- Place a few slices of artichoke hearts and cucumber on top of the mayo mixture.

- Sprinkle with salt and pepper to taste.

- Place the baking sheet in the oven and bake for 10-12 minutes, or until the cheese is melted and the hoagies are heated through.

- Serve immediately and enjoy!

Tomato and egg scramble

Prep Time: 5 minutes

Cook Time: 10 minutes

Servings: 2

Ingredients

- 2 eggs

- 1 tomato, diced

- 1 tablespoon butter or oil

- salt and pepper to taste

Directions

- Crack the eggs into a bowl and beat lightly with a fork.

- Heat the butter or oil in a pan over medium heat.

- Add the diced tomato to the pan and sauté for a few minutes until softened.

- Pour the eggs into the pan with the tomato and scramble until cooked to your desired consistency.

- Season with salt and pepper to taste.

- Serve hot and enjoy!

Spinach frittata

Prep time: 10 minutes

Cook time: 20 minutes

Servings: 6

Ingredients

- 8 large eggs

- 1 cup milk

- 1/2 cup shredded cheese (such as mozzarella or cheddar)

- 1/2 cup chopped spinach

- 1/4 cup diced onions

- 1/4 cup diced bell peppers

- 1 tablespoon olive oil

- Salt and pepper to taste

Directions

- Preheat your oven to 350°F (175°C).

- In a medium bowl, beat the eggs and milk together.

- In a large oven-safe skillet, heat the olive oil over medium heat. Add the onions and bell peppers and sauté until they are tender, about 5 minutes.

- Add the chopped spinach to the skillet and continue to cook until it is wilted, about 2 more minutes.

- Pour the egg mixture over the vegetables in the skillet. Sprinkle the shredded cheese on top.

- Cook the frittata on the stovetop until the edges start to set, about 5 minutes.

- Transfer the skillet to the oven and bake for 10-15 minutes, until the frittata is fully set and the top is lightly golden.

- Cut the frittata into wedges and serve hot. Enjoy!

Basic potatoes

Prep time: 10 mins

Cook time: 20 mins

Servings: 4

Ingredients

- 1 pound potatoes, diced

- 2 tablespoons olive oil

- 1 teaspoon salt

- 1 teaspoon pepper

Directions

- Preheat your oven to 400°F.

- Wash and dice the potatoes into small pieces.

- In a small bowl, mix together the olive oil, salt, and pepper.

- Place the diced potatoes onto a baking sheet, and drizzle the olive oil mixture over them.

- Toss the potatoes to evenly coat them in the mixture.

- Bake for 20 minutes, or until the potatoes are tender and slightly crispy.

- Serve and enjoy!

Zucchini and ricotta egg muffins

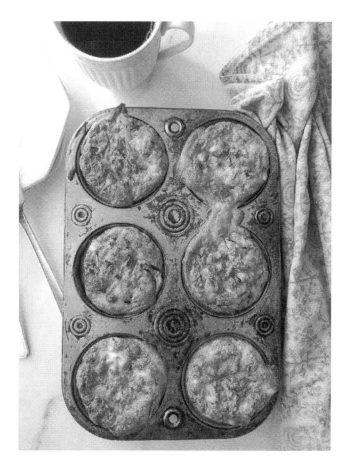

Prep time: 10 minutes

Cook time: 25 minutes

Servings: 12 muffins

Ingredients

- 1 cup grated zucchini

- 1/2 cup ricotta cheese

- 1/2 cup grated Parmesan cheese

- 3 eggs

- 1/4 cup milk

- 1/4 tsp salt

- 1/4 tsp black pepper

- 1/4 cup diced red bell pepper

- 1/4 cup diced onion

- 1/4 cup diced ham (optional)

Directions

- Preheat your oven to 350°F (175°C).

- Grate the zucchini and squeeze out any excess moisture using a cheesecloth or paper towels.

- In a large bowl, beat the eggs and mix in the ricotta, Parmesan, milk, salt, and pepper.

- Add the grated zucchini, red bell pepper, onion, and ham (if using) to the egg mixture and stir to combine.

- Lightly coat a muffin tin with cooking spray or line with muffin cups.

- Divide the mixture evenly among the muffin cups, filling each about 3/4 full.

- Bake in the preheated oven for 25 minutes, or until the muffins are set and lightly golden.

- Allow the muffins to cool in the muffin tin for a few minutes before transferring to a wire rack to cool completely. Enjoy!

Almond-cherry oatmeal bowls

Prep Time: 5 minutes

Cook Time: 5 minutes

Servings: 1

Ingredients

- 1/2 cup rolled oats

- 1 cup almond milk

- 1/4 cup chopped almonds

- 1/4 cup dried cherries

- 1 tsp honey (optional)

Directions

- In a small saucepan, bring the almond milk to a boil over medium heat.

- Add in the oats and reduce the heat to low. Cook for 5 minutes or until the oats are tender.

- Stir in the almonds and cherries.

- Sweeten with honey, if desired.

- Serve hot and enjoy!

Greek yoghurt with chocolate

Prep time: 5 minutes

Cook time: None

Servings: 1

Ingredients

- 1 cup Greek yoghurt

- 2 tbsp chocolate chips

- 1 tsp honey (optional)

Directions

- In a small bowl, microwave the chocolate chips for 20-30 seconds until they are melted.

- Stir the melted chocolate into the Greek yoghurt.

- If desired, add a teaspoon of honey for added sweetness.

- Enjoy immediately or refrigerate until ready to serve.

Easy overnight oats

Prep time: 5 minutes

Cook time: 0 minutes

Servings: 1

Ingredients

- 1/2 cup rolled oats

- 1/2 cup milk (dairy or non-dairy)

- 1/2 cup yogurt (dairy or non-dairy)

- 1 tsp sweetener (honey, maple syrup, or sugar)

- 1/2 tsp vanilla extract

- 1/2 cup fruit (fresh or frozen)

- Optional toppings: nuts, seeds, or additional fruit

Directions

- In a small bowl or jar, mix together the oats, milk, yogurt, sweetener, and vanilla extract.

- Stir in the fruit of your choice.

- Cover the bowl or jar and refrigerate overnight.

- In the morning, top with any desired toppings and enjoy cold or microwave for 1-2 minutes until warm.

Creamy blueberry-pecan overnight oats

Prep time: 5 minutes

Cook time: none

Servings: 1

Ingredients

- 1/2 cup old-fashioned oats

- 1/2 cup milk

- 1/2 cup plain yogurt

- 1/4 cup blueberries

- 1 tablespoon chopped pecans

- 1 tablespoon honey

Directions

- In a jar or small container, combine the oats, milk, yogurt, blueberries, pecans, and honey. Stir until well combined.

- Cover the jar or container with a lid and place in the refrigerator overnight.

- In the morning, remove the jar from the fridge and enjoy the oats cold or heat them up in the microwave for a warm breakfast option.

Chia pudding topped with berries

Prep Time: 5 minutes

Cook Time: 2 hours (refrigeration time)

Servings: 2

Ingredients

- 1 cup unsweetened almond milk

- 2 tablespoons chia seeds

- 1 teaspoon honey or maple syrup (optional)

- 1 teaspoon vanilla extract

- 1 cup mixed berries (such as strawberries, blueberries, and raspberries)

Directions

- In a medium bowl, whisk together the almond milk, chia seeds, honey or maple syrup (if using), and vanilla extract until well combined.

- Cover the bowl and refrigerate for at least 2 hours, or overnight.

- When ready to serve, divide the chia pudding between two bowls and top with the mixed berries.

- Enjoy immediately.

- Muesli with raspberries

Fig Bowl

Prep Time: 15 minutes

Cook Time: 20 minutes

Servings: 4

Ingredients

- 1 cup quinoa

- 2 cups water

- 1 red bell pepper, diced

- 1 cup cherry tomatoes, halved

- 1/2 cup black beans, drained and rinsed

- 1/4 cup diced red onion

- 1/4 cup diced cucumber

- 2 tbsp diced jalapeno

- 1/4 cup chopped cilantro

- 1/4 cup chopped parsley

- 2 tbsp olive oil

- 1 tsp cumin

- 1 tsp chili powder

- 1/2 tsp salt

- 1/2 tsp black pepper

- juice of 1 lime

Directions

- Rinse the quinoa in a fine-mesh sieve under cold running water. Add the quinoa and water to a medium saucepan and bring to a boil over high heat. Reduce the heat to low and simmer, covered, until the quinoa is tender and the water is absorbed, about 20 minutes.

- Meanwhile, in a large bowl, combine the bell pepper, cherry tomatoes, black beans, red onion, cucumber, jalapeno, cilantro, and parsley.

- In a small bowl, whisk together the olive oil, cumin, chili powder, salt, black pepper, and lime juice.

- Fluff the cooked quinoa with a fork and add it to the large bowl with the vegetables. Pour the dressing over the top and toss to combine.

Serve immediately, or chill in the refrigerator for a few hours for a cold fig bowl. Enjoy!

Lunch

Baked cauliflower au gratin

Prep time: 15 minutes

Cook time: 40 minutes

Servings: 6

Ingredients

- 1 large head of cauliflower, cut into florets

- 1 cup heavy cream

- 1 cup grated cheddar cheese

- 1/2 cup grated parmesan cheese

- 2 cloves garlic, minced

- 1 tsp salt

- 1/2 tsp black pepper

- 1/4 tsp paprika

- 1/4 cup breadcrumbs

Directions

- Preheat your oven to 400°F (200°C).

- In a large pot of boiling salted water, cook the cauliflower florets for 5-6 minutes until tender but still firm. Drain and set aside.

- In a medium saucepan, heat the heavy cream over medium heat until it comes to a simmer. Stir in the garlic, salt, pepper, and paprika.

- Add in the grated cheddar cheese and parmesan cheese, stirring until the cheese is melted and the sauce is smooth.

- Transfer the cauliflower to a greased baking dish and pour the cheese sauce over the top. Sprinkle the breadcrumbs over the top.

- Bake the cauliflower au gratin in the preheated oven for 20-25 minutes, until the top is golden brown and bubbly.

- Serve hot and enjoy!

Greek salad with avocados

Prep time: 15 minutes

Cook time: 0 minutes

Servings: 4

Ingredients

- 1 large tomato, diced

- 1 large cucumber, diced

- 1/2 red onion, thinly sliced

- 1/2 cup pitted kalamata olives

- 1/4 cup crumbled feta cheese

- 2 avocados, peeled and diced

- 2 tablespoons red wine vinegar

- 4 tablespoons olive oil

- salt and pepper to taste

Directions

- In a large bowl, combine the tomato, cucumber, red onion, olives, and feta cheese.

- Add in the diced avocados.

- In a small bowl, whisk together the red wine vinegar, olive oil, salt, and pepper.

- Pour the dressing over the salad and toss to coat.

- Serve immediately and enjoy!

Greek roasted vegetables

Prep time: 15 minutes

Cook time: 45 minutes

Servings: 4

Ingredients

- 1 pound small potatoes, halved

- 1 large red bell pepper, diced

- 1 large yellow bell pepper, diced

- 1 small zucchini, diced

- 1 small yellow squash, diced

- 1/2 red onion, diced

- 2 cloves garlic, minced

- 2 tablespoons olive oil

- 1 teaspoon dried oregano

- 1/2 teaspoon salt

- 1/4 teaspoon black pepper

Directions

- Preheat your oven to 400 degrees Fahrenheit.

- In a large mixing bowl, combine the potatoes, bell peppers, zucchini, yellow squash, red onion, and garlic.

- Drizzle the vegetables with olive oil and sprinkle with the oregano, salt, and black pepper. Toss to coat the vegetables evenly.

- Spread the vegetables out in a single layer on a baking sheet.

- Roast in the preheated oven for 45 minutes, or until the vegetables are tender and starting to brown.

- Serve the roasted vegetables hot, garnished with additional oregano and a sprinkle of salt if desired. Enjoy!

Potatoes and cucumbers

Prep Time: 15 minutes

Cook Time: 15 minutes

Servings: 4

Ingredients

- 4 potatoes, cut into small cubes

- 1 cucumber, sliced

- 1 tablespoon olive oil

- Salt and pepper to taste

Directions

- Preheat your oven to 400 degrees F.

- Place the cubed potatoes on a baking sheet and drizzle with olive oil. Toss to coat.

- Bake the potatoes for 15 minutes, or until they are tender and golden brown.

- In the meantime, slice the cucumber into thin slices.

- Once the potatoes are done, remove them from the oven and place them in a serving dish.

- Add the sliced cucumber to the dish and season with salt and pepper to taste.

- Serve and enjoy!

Basil Salmon

Prep Time: 15 minutes

Cook Time: 20 minutes

Servings: 4

Ingredients

- 4 salmon fillets

- 1/4 cup olive oil

- 1 lemon, juiced

- 1 tsp garlic powder

- 1 tsp dried basil

- Salt and pepper to taste

Directions

- Preheat your oven to 400 degrees F.

- In a small bowl, mix together the olive oil, lemon juice, garlic powder, and dried basil.

- Place the salmon fillets in a baking dish and brush with the olive oil mixture.

- Season with salt and pepper to taste.

- Bake in the preheated oven for 20 minutes, or until the salmon is cooked through and flakes easily with a fork.

- Serve immediately with your choice of sides and enjoy!

Chicken Gyros

Prep Time: 20 minutes

Cook Time: 10 minutes

Servings: 4

Ingredients

- 4 chicken breasts

- 1 cup Greek yogurt

- 1 lemon, juiced

- 1 tsp garlic powder

- 1 tsp paprika

- 1 tsp cumin

- 1 tsp dried oregano

- 1 tsp dried thyme

- Salt and pepper, to taste

- 4 pita breads

- 1 cup thinly sliced red onions

- 1 cup thinly sliced tomatoes

- 1 cup crumbled feta cheese

- 1 cup chopped lettuce

- 1 cup tzatziki sauce

Directions

- Preheat your grill to medium-high heat.

- In a small bowl, mix together the Greek yogurt, lemon juice, garlic powder, paprika, cumin, oregano, thyme, and a pinch of salt and pepper.

- Place the chicken breasts in a shallow dish and coat with the yogurt mixture. Let marinate for 10-15 minutes.

- Grill the chicken for 5-6 minutes on each side, or until fully cooked.

- Thinly slice the grilled chicken.

- Warm the pita breads on the grill or in the oven for a few minutes.

- Assemble the gyros by placing a few slices of chicken on each pita bread, then top with red onions, tomatoes, feta cheese, lettuce, and tzatziki sauce.

- Serve immediately.

Greek Style Salad

Prep time: 20 minutes

Cook time: 0 minutes

Servings: 4

Ingredients

- 1 head of romaine lettuce, chopped

- 1 pint cherry tomatoes, halved

- 1/2 English cucumber, diced

- 1/2 cup pitted Kalamata olives

- 1/4 cup red onion, thinly sliced

- 1/2 cup crumbled feta cheese

- 1/4 cup olive oil

- 2 tablespoons red wine vinegar

- 1 garlic clove, minced

- 1/2 teaspoon dried oregano

- Salt and pepper to taste

Directions

- In a large bowl, combine the chopped lettuce, cherry tomatoes, cucumber, olives, and red onion.

- In a separate small bowl, whisk together the olive oil, red wine vinegar, minced garlic, oregano, salt, and pepper.

- Pour the dressing over the salad and toss to evenly coat.

- Sprinkle the crumbled feta cheese over the top of the salad.

- Serve immediately and enjoy!

Brown rice salad with cheese

Prep time: 20 minutes

Cook time: 45 minutes

Servings: 4

Ingredients

- 1 cup brown rice

- 1 cup grated cheese (such as cheddar or feta)

- 1/2 cup diced tomatoes

- 1/2 cup diced cucumbers

- 1/4 cup diced red onions

- 1/4 cup diced bell peppers

- 1/4 cup chopped fresh herbs (such as parsley or basil)

- 1/4 cup olive oil

- 2 tbsp red wine vinegar

- Salt and pepper to taste

Directions

- Rinse the brown rice and place it in a pot with 2 cups of water. Bring to a boil, then reduce the heat to low and let it simmer for 45 minutes, or until the rice is cooked and tender.

- Meanwhile, dice the tomatoes, cucumbers, red onions, and bell peppers. Chop the fresh herbs.

- In a small bowl, whisk together the olive oil, red wine vinegar, salt, and pepper to make a dressing.

- Once the rice is cooked, drain any excess water and transfer it to a large bowl. Add the grated cheese, diced vegetables, and chopped herbs. Toss everything together until well combined.

- Drizzle the dressing over the top of the salad and toss to coat. Serve immediately, or refrigerate until ready to serve.

Halibut Sandwiches

Prep time: 15 minutes

Cook time: 10 minutes

Servings: 4 sandwiches

Ingredients

- 1 lb halibut fillets

- 2 tbsp olive oil

- Salt and pepper

- 4 sandwich rolls

- 4 slices of tomato

- 4 leaves of lettuce

- 1/2 cup mayonnaise

- 4 slices of cheese (optional)

Directions

- Preheat a grill or grill pan over medium-high heat.

- Brush the halibut fillets with olive oil and season with salt and pepper.

- Grill the halibut for 5-7 minutes on each side, or until it is cooked through and flakes easily with a fork.

- Assemble the sandwiches by spreading mayonnaise on the sandwich rolls, then adding the grilled halibut, tomato, lettuce, and cheese (if using).

- Serve immediately. Enjoy!

Mediterranean tuna-spinach salad

Prep Time: 15 minutes

Cook Time: 5 minutes

Servings: 4

Ingredients

- 8 oz canned tuna, drained

- 4 cups baby spinach

- 1 cup cherry tomatoes, halved

- 1/2 cup sliced red onion

- 1/2 cup sliced cucumber

- 1/2 cup sliced bell pepper

- 1/2 cup kalamata olives

- 1/4 cup crumbled feta cheese

- 2 tbsp olive oil

- 1 tbsp red wine vinegar

- 1 tsp dried oregano

- salt and pepper to taste

Directions

- In a large mixing bowl, combine the tuna, spinach, cherry tomatoes, red onion, cucumber, bell pepper, and olives.

- In a small bowl, whisk together the olive oil, red wine vinegar, oregano, salt, and pepper.

- Pour the dressing over the salad and toss to combine.

- Sprinkle the feta cheese over the top of the salad.

Dijon salmon with green bean pilaf

Prep time: 10 minutes

Cook time: 15 minutes

Servings: 4

Ingredients

- 4 salmon fillets

- 1 tbsp Dijon mustard

- 1 tbsp honey

- Salt and pepper to taste

- 1 tbsp olive oil

- 1 cup green beans, trimmed and cut into 1-inch pieces

- 1 cup basmati rice

- 2 cups water

- 1 tbsp butter

- 2 cloves garlic, minced

- 1 tbsp chopped fresh parsley

Directions

- Preheat your oven to 400°F.

- In a small bowl, mix together the Dijon mustard, honey, salt and pepper. Brush the mixture onto the salmon fillets.

- Heat the olive oil in a large skillet over medium heat. Add the salmon fillets and cook for 3-4 minutes on each side, or until they are browned and cooked through.

- Transfer the salmon to a baking sheet and place it in the preheated oven for 5-7 minutes, or until it is cooked to your desired level of doneness.

- While the salmon is cooking, prepare the green bean pilaf. Rinse the basmati rice in a fine-mesh sieve until the water runs clear.

- In a medium saucepan, bring the water to a boil. Add the butter and rice, and reduce the heat to low. Cover the pan and simmer for 18-20 minutes, or until the rice is tender and the water has been absorbed.

- In a small skillet, heat the garlic in a little bit of olive oil over medium heat until it is fragrant. Add the green beans and cook for 2-3 minutes, or until they are tender.

- Stir the green beans and garlic into the cooked rice. Sprinkle with fresh parsley before serving.

- Serve the salmon with the green bean pilaf on the side. Enjoy!

Meal-prep falafel bowls with tahini sauce

Prep time: 30 minutes

Cook time: 15 minutes

Servings: 4

Ingredients

- 1 cup dried chickpeas, soaked in water overnight

- 1 small onion, minced

- 3 cloves garlic, minced

- 1/2 cup parsley, chopped

- 1/2 cup cilantro, chopped

- 1 tsp cumin

- 1 tsp coriander

- 1 tsp salt

- 1/2 tsp black pepper

- 2 tbsp flour

- 1 cup tahini sauce

- 4 cups cooked quinoa or rice

- 4 cups mixed vegetables, such as diced tomatoes, cucumbers, and bell peppers

Directions

- Preheat your oven to 375°F.

- In a food processor, combine the soaked and drained chickpeas, onion, garlic, parsley, cilantro, cumin, coriander, salt, and pepper. Pulse until the mixture is well combined and starts to form a paste.

- Scoop spoonfuls of the falafel mixture onto a baking sheet lined with parchment paper, and flatten each ball slightly with the back of a spoon.

- Bake the falafel for 15-20 minutes, or until golden brown.

- Meanwhile, prepare your quinoa or rice according to package instructions.

- In a small bowl, whisk together the tahini sauce with a few tablespoons of water until it reaches your desired consistency.

- To assemble the bowls, divide the quinoa or rice, mixed vegetables, and falafel evenly among four bowls.

- Drizzle the tahini sauce over the top of each bowl, and serve.

Balsamic roasted chicken and vegetables

Prep Time: 10 minutes

Cook Time: 45 minutes

Servings: 4

Ingredients

- 4 chicken breasts

- 2 bell peppers, diced

- 1 onion, diced

- 2 cups cherry tomatoes

- 2 tbsp olive oil

- 2 tbsp balsamic vinegar

- 1 tsp salt

- 1 tsp pepper

- 1 tsp garlic powder

- 1 tsp dried basil

Directions

- Preheat your oven to 400°F (200°C).

- In a large mixing bowl, combine the diced bell peppers, onion, cherry tomatoes, olive oil, balsamic vinegar, salt, pepper, garlic powder, and dried basil. Mix well to evenly coat the vegetables.

- Place the chicken breasts in a baking dish and pour the vegetables around them.

- Roast in the preheated oven for 45 minutes, or until the chicken is cooked through and the vegetables are tender.

Brussels sprouts salad with crispy chickpeas

Prep time: 20 minutes

Cook time: 15 minutes

Servings: 4

Ingredients

- 1 lb Brussels sprouts, trimmed and thinly sliced

- 1 can chickpeas, drained and rinsed

- 1 tbsp olive oil

- 1/4 tsp salt

- 1/4 tsp black pepper

- 1/4 cup crumbled feta cheese

- 1/4 cup chopped toasted almonds

- 1/4 cup chopped fresh parsley

Dressing

- 2 tbsp olive oil

- 1 tbsp dijon mustard

- 1 tbsp honey

- 1 tbsp apple cider vinegar

- 1/4 tsp salt

- 1/4 tsp black pepper

Directions

- Preheat the oven to 400°F. Spread the chickpeas onto a baking sheet and toss with the olive oil, salt, and pepper. Roast in the oven for 15 minutes or until crispy.

- In a small bowl, whisk together the dressing ingredients.

- In a large bowl, combine the Brussels sprouts, crispy chickpeas, feta cheese, almonds, and parsley. Toss with the dressing until well coated.

- Serve the salad immediately or refrigerate until ready to serve. Enjoy!

Vegetarian spaghetti squash lasagna

Prep Time: 20 minutes

Cook Time: 1 hour

Servings: 4

Ingredients

- 1 medium spaghetti squash

- 1 cup marinara sauce

- 1 cup diced vegetables (such as bell peppers, mushrooms, and zucchini)

- 1 cup crumbled tofu or sliced tempeh

- 1 cup grated vegan cheese

- Fresh herbs for garnish (optional)

Directions

- Preheat your oven to 350°F (180°C).

- Cut the spaghetti squash in half lengthwise and scoop out the seeds. Place the squash cut-side down on a baking sheet lined with parchment paper.

- Bake the squash for 35-40 minutes or until the flesh is tender and can easily be shredded with a fork.

- While the squash is cooking, heat a pan over medium heat and add the diced vegetables. Cook until they are tender, about 5-7 minutes.

- Remove the squash from the oven and use a fork to shred the flesh into spaghetti-like strands.

- In a baking dish, layer the squash, marinara sauce, diced vegetables, crumbled tofu or tempeh, and grated vegan cheese. Repeat until all ingredients are used up, ending with a layer of cheese on top.

- Bake the lasagna for 25-30 minutes or until the cheese is melted and bubbly.

- Garnish with fresh herbs and serve hot. Enjoy!

Garlic and artichoke pasta

Prep Time: 10 minutes

Cook Time: 20 minutes

Servings: 4

Ingredients

- 8 ounces (226 grams, 05 pound) spaghetti or linguine

- 2 tablespoons olive oil

- 1 small onion, diced

- 3 cloves garlic, minced

- 1 can diced tomatoes

- 1 can quartered artichoke hearts, drained

- 2 tablespoons chopped fresh parsley

- salt and pepper to taste

Directions

- Bring a pot of salted water to a boil and cook pasta according to package instructions.

- In a separate pan, heat olive oil over medium heat. Add onion and garlic and sauté until onion is translucent, about 5 minutes.

- Add diced tomatoes and artichoke hearts to the pan and cook for an additional 5 minutes.

- Add parsley, salt, and pepper to the pan and stir to combine.

- Drain the pasta and add it to the pan with the sauce. Toss the pasta until it is well coated with the sauce.

- Serve hot and enjoy!

Spaghetti with tomato and basil

Prep time: 15 mins

Cook time: 15 mins

Servings: 4

Ingredients

- 1 pound spaghetti

- 2 tablespoons olive oil

- 1 small onion, diced

- 2 cloves garlic, minced

- 1 (14.5 ounce, 411 grams, 0,9 pound) can diced tomatoes

- 1/2 cup fresh basil, chopped

- salt and pepper to taste

Directions

- Bring a large pot of salted water to a boil. Add the spaghetti and cook according to package instructions until al dente.

- In a separate pan, heat the olive oil over medium heat. Add the onion and garlic and sauté until the onion is translucent.

- Add the diced tomatoes to the pan and bring to a simmer. Reduce heat to low and let the sauce cook for about 10 minutes.

- Stir in the fresh basil and season with salt and pepper to taste.

- Drain the spaghetti and add it to the pan with the tomato sauce. Toss to coat the spaghetti in the sauce.

- Serve the spaghetti hot and garnish with additional fresh basil if desired.

Spaghetti with brown butter and feta

Prep time: 10 minutes

Cook time: 10 minutes

Servings: 2

Ingredients

- 1/2 pound spaghetti

- 2 tablespoons unsalted butter

- 2 cloves garlic, minced

- 1/4 cup crumbled feta cheese

- Salt and pepper to taste

- Fresh parsley for garnish (optional)

Directions

- Bring a large pot of salted water to a boil and cook spaghetti according to package instructions.

- In a separate pan, melt the butter over medium heat. Cook until the butter turns a golden brown color, stirring occasionally.

- Add the minced garlic and cook for another minute until fragrant.

- Drain the spaghetti and add it to the pan with the brown butter and garlic. Toss to coat.

- Add the crumbled feta cheese and toss again.

- Season with salt and pepper to taste.

- Garnish with fresh parsley, if desired, and serve hot.

Spaghetti with Mushroom ragu

Prep Time: 15 minutes

Cook Time: 45 minutes

Servings: 4

Ingredients

- 1 pound spaghetti

- 1 tablespoon olive oil

- 1 small onion, diced

- 1 garlic clove, minced

- 8 ounces (226 grams, 0,5 pound) cremini mushrooms, sliced

- 1 cup tomato sauce

- 1/2 cup water

- 2 tablespoons tomato paste

- 1 teaspoon dried oregano

- 1/2 teaspoon salt

- 1/4 teaspoon black pepper

- 1/4 cup chopped fresh parsley

Directions

- Bring a large pot of salted water to a boil. Add the spaghetti and cook according to package instructions. Drain and set aside.

- In a large saucepan, heat the olive oil over medium heat. Add the onion and cook until it is soft and translucent, about 5 minutes.

- Add the garlic and mushrooms to the saucepan and cook until the mushrooms are tender, about 5 more minutes.

- Stir in the tomato sauce, water, tomato paste, oregano, salt, and pepper. Reduce the heat to low and simmer for 30 minutes.

- Add the cooked spaghetti to the saucepan and toss to coat with the mushroom ragu.

- Serve the spaghetti topped with fresh parsley. Enjoy!

Spaghetti with green bean

Prep Time: 15 mins

Cook Time: 20 mins

Servings: 4

Ingredients

- 8 ounces (226 grams, 0,5 pound) spaghetti

- 1 pound green beans, trimmed

- 2 cloves garlic, minced

- 1 tablespoon olive oil

- Salt and pepper to taste

Directions

- Bring a large pot of salted water to a boil. Add the spaghetti and cook according to package instructions until al dente.

- In the last 3 minutes of cooking the spaghetti, add the green beans to the pot.

- Drain the spaghetti and green beans in a colander, reserving 1/2 cup of the cooking water.

- In a large skillet, heat the olive oil over medium heat. Add the garlic and sauté for 1 minute until fragrant.

- Add the spaghetti and green beans to the skillet and toss with the garlic and oil. Season with salt and pepper to taste.

- If the mixture seems dry, add a splash of the reserved cooking water to loosen it up.

- Serve hot and enjoy!

Penne all'arrabbiata

Prep time: 10 minutes

Cook time: 15 minutes

Servings: 4

Ingredients

- 16 ounces (1 pound, 453 grams) penne pasta

- 1 tablespoon olive oil

- 1 medium onion, diced

- 3 cloves garlic, minced

- 1 teaspoon red pepper flakes

- 1 (28-ounce, 793 grams, 1,75 pound) can crushed tomatoes

- 1/2 cup water

- 1/2 teaspoon salt

- 1/4 teaspoon black pepper

- 1/4 cup chopped fresh parsley

- 1/4 cup grated Parmesan cheese

Directions

- Bring a large pot of salted water to a boil. Add the pasta and cook according to package instructions until al dente. Drain and set aside.

- In a large saucepan, heat the olive oil over medium heat. Add the onions and garlic and cook until the onions are translucent, about 5 minutes.

- Add the red pepper flakes, crushed tomatoes, water, salt, and black pepper to the saucepan. Bring to a boil, then reduce the heat to low and simmer for 10 minutes.

- Stir in the cooked pasta, parsley, and Parmesan cheese. Serve hot.

Lemon couscous with broccoli

Prep time: 10 minutes

Cook time: 15 minutes

Servings: 4

Ingredients

- 1 cup couscous

- 1 cup water

- 1 lemon, juiced

- 1 head of broccoli, cut into florets

- 2 tablespoons olive oil

- salt and pepper to taste

Directions

- In a small pot, bring the water to a boil. Add the couscous and turn off the heat. Cover the pot and let it sit for 5 minutes.

- Fluff the couscous with a fork and stir in the lemon juice. Set aside.

- In a separate pan, heat the olive oil over medium heat. Add the broccoli florets and cook for 5-7 minutes, or until tender.

- Add the cooked broccoli to the couscous and stir to combine. Season with salt and pepper to taste.

- Serve the couscous and broccoli hot. Enjoy!

Mint brown rice

Prep time: 10 minutes

Cook time: 45 minutes

Servings: 4

Ingredients

- 1 cup brown rice

- 2 cups water

- 1 tablespoon butter

- 1/4 cup mint leaves, finely chopped

Directions

- Rinse the brown rice in a fine mesh sieve until the water runs clear.

- In a medium saucepan, bring the water to a boil.

- Add the rinsed rice and butter to the saucepan, and stir to combine.

- Reduce the heat to low and simmer, covered, for 45 minutes or until the rice is tender and the water has been absorbed.

- Once the rice is cooked, stir in the finely chopped mint leaves.

- Serve the rice hot and enjoy!

Mediterranean lentils

Prep time: 15 minutes

Cook time: 45 minutes

Servings: 4

Ingredients

- 1 cup dried lentils

- 2 cups water

- 1/2 cup diced onion

- 1/2 cup diced carrot

- 1/2 cup diced celery

- 1 clove garlic, minced

- 1 teaspoon ground cumin

- 1 teaspoon ground coriander

- 1/2 teaspoon paprika

- 1/4 teaspoon ground cinnamon

- 1/4 teaspoon ground allspice

- 1/4 teaspoon ground black pepper

- 1/4 teaspoon salt

- 2 tablespoons tomato paste

- 1 can diced tomatoes, undrained

- 1/2 cup chopped fresh parsley

- 1/4 cup chopped fresh mint

Directions

- Rinse lentils and place in a saucepan with water. Bring to a boil, then reduce heat to low and simmer for 25-30 minutes, or until lentils are tender.

- Meanwhile, in a large skillet, heat a small amount of oil over medium heat. Add onions, carrots, celery, and garlic and sauté until vegetables are tender, about 5-7 minutes.

- Stir in cumin, coriander, paprika, cinnamon, allspice, black pepper, and salt. Add tomato paste and diced tomatoes, and bring to a simmer.

- Drain lentils and add them to the skillet. Cook for an additional 10 minutes, or until heated through.

- Stir in parsley and mint, and serve hot. Enjoy!

Cauliflower risotto with mushrooms

Prep time: 10 minutes

Cook time: 20 minutes

Servings: 4

Ingredients

- 1 head of cauliflower

- 1 tbsp olive oil

- 1 small onion, diced

- 1 cup sliced mushrooms

- 1 clove garlic, minced

- 1/2 cup Arborio rice

- 2 cups vegetable broth

- 1/2 cup white wine

- 1 tbsp butter

- 1/4 cup parmesan cheese, grated

- salt and pepper to taste

Directions

- Wash and dry the cauliflower, then pulse it in a food processor until it is in small, rice-like pieces.

- In a large saucepan, heat the olive oil over medium heat. Add the diced onion and sauté for 2-3 minutes until it is translucent.

- Add the mushrooms and garlic to the pan and cook for another 2-3 minutes until the mushrooms are soft.

- Add the Arborio rice to the pan and stir to coat it in the oil and vegetables. Cook for 1-2 minutes until the rice is slightly toasted.

- Pour in the vegetable broth and white wine, stirring to combine. Bring the mixture to a boil, then reduce the heat to low and simmer for 15-20 minutes, stirring occasionally, until the rice is cooked and the liquid is absorbed.

- Once the rice is cooked, stir in the butter and parmesan cheese until the cheese is melted. Season with salt and pepper to taste.

- Serve the cauliflower rice risotto hot, garnished with additional parmesan cheese if desired. Enjoy!

Vegetable and tofu scramble

Prep time: 10 minutes

Cook time: 10 minutes

Servings: 2

Ingredients

- 1/2 block firm tofu, crumbled

- 1/2 small onion, diced

- 1 small bell pepper, diced

- 1 small tomato, diced

- 1 cup spinach, chopped

- 1 tsp olive oil

- 1 tsp turmeric

- 1 tsp cumin

- Salt and pepper to taste

Directions

- Heat the olive oil in a pan over medium heat.

- Add the onion and bell pepper to the pan and sauté until they are soft, about 5 minutes.

- Add the crumbled tofu, turmeric, cumin, salt and pepper to the pan. Stir until the tofu is coated in the spices.

- Add the tomato and spinach to the pan and stir until they are wilted.

- Serve the vegetable and tofu scramble hot.

Parmesan asparagus with tomatoes

Prep time: 5 minutes

Cook time: 10 minutes

Servings: 4

Ingredients

- 1 bunch of asparagus, trimmed

- 1 pint cherry tomatoes, halved

- 2 tablespoons olive oil

- 2 tablespoons grated parmesan cheese

- Salt and pepper to taste

Directions

- Preheat the oven to 400°F.

- Place the asparagus and cherry tomatoes on a baking sheet. Drizzle with olive oil and sprinkle with salt and pepper.

- Roast in the oven for 10 minutes, or until the asparagus is tender.

- Sprinkle the grated parmesan cheese over the top of the vegetables and return to the oven for an additional 2 minutes, or until the cheese is melted and slightly browned.

- Serve hot and enjoy!

Linguine with tapenade

Prep Time: 10 minutes

Cook Time: 15 minutes

Servings: 4

Ingredients

- 8 ounces (0,5 pound, 226 grams) linguine

- 1/4 cup olive oil

- 1/4 cup black olives, pitted and chopped

- 1/4 cup green olives, pitted and chopped

- 2 cloves garlic, minced

- 1/4 cup capers

- 1/4 cup fresh parsley, chopped

- 2 tablespoons red wine vinegar

- Salt and pepper to taste

Directions

- Cook the linguine according to the package instructions.

- In a small pan, heat the olive oil over medium heat. Add the black olives, green olives, garlic, and capers. Cook for 2-3 minutes until the garlic is fragrant.

- Add the parsley and red wine vinegar to the pan and stir to combine.

- Drain the cooked linguine and add it to the pan with the tapenade. Toss to coat the linguine evenly.

- Season with salt and pepper to taste. Serve hot.

Shrimp, macaroni and feta

Prep time: 15 minutes

Cook time: 15 minutes

Servings: 4

Ingredients

- 8 oz uncooked elbow macaroni

- 1 lb medium shrimp, peeled and deveined

- 1 tbsp olive oil

- 1/2 cup diced onion

- 2 cloves garlic, minced

- 1/2 cup tomato sauce

- 1/4 cup crumbled feta cheese

- Salt and pepper to taste

Directions

- Cook the macaroni according to package instructions. Drain and set aside.

- Heat the olive oil in a large skillet over medium heat. Add the onion and garlic and cook until the onion is translucent, about 5 minutes.

- Add the shrimp to the skillet and cook until they are pink, about 3-4 minutes per side.

- Add the tomato sauce and cooked macaroni to the skillet and stir to combine.

- Sprinkle the crumbled feta cheese over the top of the dish and season with salt and pepper to taste.

- Serve hot and enjoy!

Fusilli with Italian pesto Genovese

Prep time: 10 minutes

Cook time: 8 minutes

Servings: 4

Ingredients

- 8 ounces fusilli pasta

- 1 cup Italian pesto Genovese sauce

- 1/4 cup grated Parmesan cheese

- Salt and pepper to taste

Directions

- Bring a large pot of salted water to a boil. Add the fusilli pasta and cook according to package instructions.

- Drain the pasta and return it to the pot. Add the Italian pesto Genovese sauce and stir until the pasta is well coated.

- Sprinkle the grated Parmesan cheese over the pasta and stir to combine.

- Season with salt and pepper to taste.

- Serve the pasta hot and enjoy!

Greek-style rigatoni

Prep time: 15 minutes

Cook time: 15 minutes

Servings: 4

Ingredients

- 8 ounces (0,5 pound, 226 grams) rigatoni pasta

- 1 tablespoon olive oil

- 1 small onion, diced

- 1 red bell pepper, diced

- 1 yellow bell pepper, diced

- 1 cup cherry tomatoes, halved

- 1/2 cup diced cooked chicken

- 1/2 cup crumbled feta cheese

- 1/4 cup diced Kalamata olives

- 1/4 cup chopped fresh parsley

- 1/4 cup chopped fresh mint

- 1/4 cup chopped fresh basil

- Salt and pepper to taste

Directions

- Bring a pot of salted water to a boil and cook the rigatoni according to the package instructions. Drain and set aside.

- In a large skillet, heat the olive oil over medium heat. Add the onion and bell peppers and cook until they are soft, about 5 minutes.

- Add the cherry tomatoes, chicken, feta cheese, olives, parsley, mint, and basil to the skillet and stir to combine.

- Add the cooked rigatoni to the skillet and stir to coat the pasta with the sauce.

- Season with salt and pepper to taste and serve hot. Enjoy!

Rosemary barley with walnuts

Prep time: 10 minutes

Cook time: 45 minutes

Servings: 4

Ingredients

- 1 cup pearl barley

- 2 cups chicken broth

- 1 cup water

- 2 tablespoons olive oil

- 1 cup chopped walnuts

- 2 tablespoons chopped fresh rosemary

- salt and pepper to taste

Directions

- Rinse the pearl barley in a fine mesh strainer and set aside.

- In a medium saucepan, bring the chicken broth and water to a boil. Add the pearl barley and reduce the heat to a simmer. Cover and cook for 45 minutes, or until the barley is tender.

- In a separate pan, heat the olive oil over medium heat. Add the chopped walnuts and cook until they are toasted and fragrant, about 5 minutes.

- Once the barley is finished cooking, drain any excess liquid. Add the toasted walnuts and chopped rosemary to the pan with the barley and stir to combine. Season with salt and pepper to taste.

- Serve the rosemary barley with walnuts hot, either as a side dish or a main course. Enjoy!

Grilled salmon with roasted cauliflower

Prep Time: 15 minutes

Cook Time: 20 minutes

Servings: 4

Ingredients

- 4 salmon fillets

- 1 head of cauliflower, cut into florets

- 2 tablespoons olive oil

- Salt and pepper to taste

- 2 cloves garlic, minced

- 2 tablespoons lemon juice

- 2 tablespoons chopped fresh parsley

Directions

- Preheat your grill to medium-high heat.

- In a large bowl, toss the cauliflower florets with the olive oil, salt, and pepper. Arrange the florets on a sheet pan and roast in the oven at 400°F for 15-20 minutes, until tender and caramelized.

- While the cauliflower is roasting, season the salmon fillets with salt and pepper. Grill the salmon for about 5-7 minutes per side, until the flesh is opaque and flakes easily.

- In a small bowl, mix together the minced garlic, lemon juice, and parsley.

- Serve the grilled salmon with the roasted cauliflower and a drizzle of the garlic-lemon sauce. Enjoy!

Eggs in tomato sauce with chickpeas & Spinach

Prep Time: 15 minutes

Cook Time: 30 minutes

Servings: 4

Ingredients

- 1 tablespoon olive oil

- 1 medium onion, diced

- 3 cloves garlic, minced

- 1 can diced tomatoes

- 1 cup cooked chickpeas

- 4 large eggs

- 1 cup spinach, roughly chopped

- Salt and pepper, to taste

Directions

- Heat the olive oil in a large skillet over medium heat. Add the onion and garlic and cook until the onion is translucent, about 5 minutes.

- Add the diced tomatoes and chickpeas to the skillet and bring to a simmer.

- Crack the eggs into the skillet, spacing them evenly apart. Cover the skillet and cook until the eggs are set, about 5-7 minutes.

- Stir in the spinach and cook until it is wilted, about 2-3 minutes.

- Season with salt and pepper to taste and serve hot.

Farro salad

Prep time: 15 minutes

Cook time: 30 minutes

Servings: 4

Ingredients

- 1 cup farro

- 2 cups water

- 1/4 tsp salt

- 1 cup cherry tomatoes, halved

- 1 cup chopped cucumber

- 1/2 cup chopped red onion

- 1/2 cup chopped parsley

- 1/4 cup chopped basil

- 2 tbsp olive oil

- 1 tbsp red wine vinegar

- Salt and pepper to taste

Directions

- Rinse the farro in a fine mesh sieve and transfer to a medium saucepan. Add the water and salt and bring to a boil.

- Reduce the heat to low and simmer, covered, until the farro is tender, about 30 minutes. Drain any excess water and set aside to cool.

- In a large bowl, combine the cherry tomatoes, cucumber, red onion, parsley, and basil.

- Once the farro has cooled, add it to the bowl with the vegetables.

- In a small bowl, whisk together the olive oil and red wine vinegar. Pour over the farro and vegetables and toss to coat.

- Season with salt and pepper to taste. Serve chilled or at room temperature.

Dinner

Muffin-tin quiches with smoked cheddar & potato

Cook time: 30 mins

Servings: 6

Ingredients

- 2 tablespoons extra-virgin olive oil

- 1 ½ cups finely diced red-skinned potatoes

- 1 cup diced red onion

- ¾ teaspoon salt, divided

- 8 large eggs

- 1 cup shredded smoked Cheddar cheese

- ½ cup low-fat milk

- ½ teaspoon ground black pepper

- 1 ½ cups chopped fresh spinach

Directions

- Preheat oven to 325 degrees F. Coat a 12-cup muffin tin with cooking spray.

- Heat oil in a large skillet over medium heat. Add potatoes, onion and 1/4 teaspoon salt and cook, stirring, until the potatoes are just cooked through, about 5 minutes. Remove from heat and let cool 5 minutes.

- Whisk eggs, cheese, milk, pepper and the remaining 1/2 teaspoon salt in a large bowl. Stir in spinach and the potato mixture. Divide the quiche mixture among the prepared muffin cups.

- Bake until firm to the touch, about 25 minutes. Let stand 5 minutes before removing from the tin.

Chicken & Vegetable penne with parsley-walnut pesto

Cook time: 25 mins

Servings: 4

Ingredients

- ¾ cup chopped walnuts

- 1 cup lightly packed parsley leaves

- 2 cloves garlic, crushed and peeled

- ½ teaspoon plus 1/8 teaspoon salt

- ⅛ teaspoon ground pepper

- 2 tablespoons olive oil

- ⅓ cup grated Parmesan cheese

- 1 ½ cups shredded or sliced cooked skinless chicken breast (8 oz.)

- 6 ounces (0,37 pound, 170 grams) whole-wheat penne or fusilli pasta (1 3/4 cups)

- 8 ounces (0,5 pound, 226 grams) green beans, trimmed and halved crosswise (2 cups)

- 2 cups cauliflower florets (8 oz.)

Directions

- Bring a large pot of water to a boil.

- Place walnuts in a small bowl and microwave on High until fragrant and lightly toasted, 2 to 2 1/2 minutes. (Alternatively, toast the walnuts in a small dry skillet over medium-low heat, stirring constantly, until fragrant, 2 to 3 minutes.) Transfer to a plate and let cool. Set 1/4 cup aside for topping.

- Combine the remaining 1/2 cup walnuts, parsley, garlic, salt, and pepper in a food processor. Process until the nuts are ground. With the motor running, gradually add oil through the feed tube. Add Parmesan and pulse until mixed in. Scrape the pesto into a large bowl. Add chicken.

- Meanwhile, cook pasta in the boiling water for 4 minutes. Add green beans and cauliflower; cover and cook until the pasta is al dente (almost tender) and the vegetables are tender, 5 to 7 minutes more. Before draining, scoop out 3/4 cup of the cooking water and stir it into the pesto-chicken mixture to warm it slightly. Drain the pasta and vegetables and add to the pesto-chicken mixture. Toss to coat well. Divide among 4 pasta bowls and top each serving with 1 Tbsp. of the reserved walnuts.

Greek turkey burgers with spinach, feta & Tzatziki

Prep Time: 15 minutes

Cook Time: 10 minutes

Servings: 4 burgers

Ingredients

For the Turkey Burgers:

- 1 pound ground turkey

- ½ cup fresh spinach leaves , chopped

- ⅓ cup sun-dried tomatoes , chopped

- ¼ cup red onion , minced

- ¼ cup feta cheese , crumbled

- 2 cloves garlic , pressed or minced

- 1 egg , whisked

- 1 tablespoon olive oil

- 1 teaspoon dried oregano

- ½ teaspoon kosher salt

- ½ teaspoon freshly ground black pepper

- 4 soft whole-wheat hamburger buns

- Bibb lettuce leaves

- Sliced red onion

For the Tzatziki Sauce:

- ½ cucumber , halved with skin and seeds removed

- ¾ cup low-fat plain Greek yogurt

- 2 cloves garlic , pressed or minced

- 1 tablespoon red wine vinegar

- 1 tablespoon fresh dill , minced

- Pinch of kosher salt and freshly ground black pepper

Directions

- In a large bowl, add the ground turkey, spinach, sun-dried tomatoes, red onion and feta. In a small bowl, whisk together the garlic, egg, olive oil and dried oregano and kosher salt and freshly ground black pepper then pour over the turkey and mix with your hands to combine.

- Divide the burger mixture into 4 portions and mold into patties. Place on a cutting board or plate dividing the patties with parchment paper and refrigerated for 30 minutes up to overnight. You could also individually freeze the patties at this point for up to 3 months.

- Prepare the tzatziki sauce by grating the cucumber. Gather the cucumber together and place in a paper towel and press the water out of the shredded cucumber and place in a medium size bowl. Add the yogurt, garlic, red wine vinegar, fresh dill, kosher salt and freshly ground black pepper and mix well. Cover and refrigerate for 30 minutes or up to 3 days.

- Heat a non-stick grill pan over medium heat and spray well with cooking spray.

- Place the turkey burgers on the grill, cover with an upside down sheet pan or lid and cook for about 5 minutes per side. Be sure to watch the burgers and monitor your heat as the burgers will brown quickly if the heat is too high.

- Slather buns with tzatziki sauce and garnish with lettuce leaves and red onion. Or serve bunless in the bibb lettuce leaves.

Olive caper salmon bake

Prep Time: 20 mins

Cook Time: 30 mins

Servings: 8 people

Ingredients

- 70 ml olive oil

- 8 anchovy fillets drained and finely chopped

- 2.5 tbsp tomato paste

- 1.5 tsp chilli flakes

- 2 tsp coriander seeds lightly bashed in a mortar

- 8 cloves garlic peeled and very thinly sliced

- 2 preserved lemons flesh scooped out and discarded, rind finely chopped (60g net)

- 2 tsp mable syrup

- 1 lemon cut into 5mm-thin rounds (130g)

- 1 salmon fillet (about 1.2kg), pin-boned, skin left on

- 200 g datterini tomatoes or cherry tomatoes, halved

- Salsa

- 60 g pitted kalamata olives

- 60 g baby capers (or regular capers, roughly chopped)

- 1 preserved lemon flesh scooped out and discarded, rind thinly sliced (30g)

- 20 g basil leaves roughly chopped

- 10 g flat-leaf parsley leaves roughly chopped

- 2 tbsp olive oil

- 2 tsp lemon juice

Directions

- First make the oil. Put the oil, anchovies and tomato paste in a small saute pan on a medium heat and cook, stirring, for five minutes. Add the chilli flakes and coriander seeds, cook for another minute, until fragrant, then take off the heat and add the garlic, preserved lemon and maple syrup. Stir to combine, then leave to cool for about 15 minutes.

- Meanwhile, heat the oven to 200C (180C fan)/390F/gas 6 and line a 40cm x 30cm roasting tin with greaseproof paper. Arrange the sliced lemon all over the tray. Sprinkle the salmon with an eighth of a teaspoon of salt and plenty of black pepper on each side, lay it skin side down on top of the lemon slices, then scatter the tomato halves all around the edges.

- Pour the cooled oil and its solids over the salmon, and press the garlic slices flat against the fish's flesh. Bake for 17 minutes (or up to 20, if you prefer it more cooked), then remove and leave to rest for five minutes.

- While the salmon is baking, make the salsa. Mix the olives, capers, preserved lemon, basil and parsley leaves, olive oil and lemon juice in a small bowl, then add an eighth of a teaspoon of salt and mix again. Scatter half the salsa over the salmon and serve the fish warm or at room temperature with the rest of the salsa in a bowl on the side.

Greek couscous and lambchops

Prep time: 15 mins

Cook time: 40 mins

Servings: 4

Ingredients

- 4 lamb shoulder chops

- 1 small yellow onion (diced)

- 1 red bell pepper (diced)

- 4 garlic cloves (diced)

- 2 sprigs fresh dill

- 2 sprigs fresh oregano

- kosher salt

- black pepper

- 1 ½ cup pearl couscous

- 1 cup vegetable broth

- 15 oz can diced tomatoes

- 4 oz feta cheese (crumbled)

- 1 tsp cumin

- 1 lemon zest

- 1 tbsp Avocado oil (for searing lamb)

- 2 tbsp Olive oil (plus more for garnish)

Directions

- Dice onion and red bell peppers into a larger dice, place in prep bowl. Lightly crush garlic cloves, place in prep cup. Crumble feta by hand, if necessary. Chop oregano leaves and place in prep cup. Chop dill sprigs and place in prep cup.

- Prep sous vide to 131°. Season lamb with salt and pepper and place into a vacuum seal bag. Place crushed garlic in bag and seal tightly using a vacuum sealer (affiliate) or the water displacement method. Place bag in sous vide for 2-3 hours. If you're not cooking your lamb by sous vide, simply continue with the step below.

- When your lamb has about 15 minutes left, preheat your oven to 450°. Also preheat a 9 inch cast iron pan (affiliate) over medium heat on the stove. Add 1 tbsp olive oil to pan and allow to heat for about 30 seconds. Stir couscous into pan until it begins to toast, about 3 minutes. Remove to a heatproof bowl. Remove cast iron pan (affiliate) from heat.

- Drain can of diced tomatoes and add to pan along with oregano. Drizzle with 1 tbsp olive oil, salt, pepper and oregano. Place in center of preheated oven and cook for 10 minutes. While your veggies are roasting, bring your vegetable broth to a rolling bowl in a saucepot.

- When broth reaches a boil, add 1 tsp kosher salt, dill sprigs, lemon zest and cumin. Reduce heat to keep at a rolling (not rapid!) boil and let cook for about 5 minutes, until ready to add to pan.

- When tomatoes are nice and tender, remove pan from oven and add vegetable stock (dill sprigs removed) and toasted couscous to pan. Fold together and cover pan tightly with foil. Return to oven for 20 minutes.

- Heat another pan over medium-high heat. Add a high-heat searing oil (I used Avocado oil). Remove lamb from sous vide bag and pat dry. Sear lamb in the hot pan for 30 seconds on each side, hitting every surface twice. If your pan is sufficiently hot, it should be well seared when it's done. Remove to a pan to rest.

- Immediately add diced peppers, onions and the crushed garlic from the sous vide bag. Cook until softened, about 3 minutes. Remove from heat and place peppers and onions in heatproof prep bowl. Pick out garlic cloves and roughly chop, then add back to bowl.

- After lamb has rested 10 minutes, cut loin chops into small bite size pieces. Stir into bowl with peppers and onions, pouring in any pan drippings as well. When couscous has cooked it's 20 minutes, remove foil and add lamb-onion-pepper mix as well as capers to bowl and stir in well. Cook for an additional 5 minutes, them remove from oven.

- Add feta cheese on top and broil on high until brown, about 4-5 minutes. Remove from oven and let rest about 2 minutes. Spoon each serving into a wide bowl and finish with a spriled drizzle of olive oil. Enjoy immediately!

Veggie flatbread

Prep time: 10 mins

Cook time: 15 mins

Servings: 1

Ingredients

- ½ small red onion, sliced into thin wedges

- 2 tbsp olive oil, plus an extra drizzle, to serve

- 70g cherry tomatoes

- 200g canned chickpeas, drained

- 1 small garlic clove, crushed

- ½ tbsp tahini

- ½ lemon, zested and juiced

- 1 flatbread

- 30g mixed pitted olives

- 20g vegetarian feta, crumbled

- small handful of basil, shredded

Directions

- Heat the grill to its highest setting. Spread the onion wedges out on a baking tray and drizzle with 1 tbsp of the oil. Grill for 3-5 mins turning halfway through, then add the tomatoes to the tray, season and grill for a further 5 mins or until juicy and popping.

- Put the chickpeas in a pan with the garlic and remaining 1 tbsp oil, then heat for 5 mins before crushing the chickpeas using a potato masher. Stir through the tahini, the lemon zest and juice along with 2 tbsp water. Season.

- Warm your flatbread under the grill for a couple of minutes. Top with the crushed chickpeas, then the tomato and onion mixture. Finish with the olives, feta and basil, and a drizzle of olive oil.

Skillet shrimp

Prep time: 10 minutes

Cook time: 8-10 minutes

Ingredients

- 1 pound peeled and deveined shrimp

- 2 tablespoons olive oil

- 1 clove garlic, minced

- 1 teaspoon paprika

- 1/2 teaspoon chili powder

- salt and pepper, to taste

- 2 tablespoons butter

- 2 tablespoons lemon juice

- 1 tablespoon chopped parsley (optional)

Directions

- Heat a large skillet over medium heat. Add olive oil and garlic and cook until fragrant, about 1 minute.

- Add the paprika, chili powder, salt, and pepper to the skillet and stir to combine.

- Add the shrimp to the skillet and cook until pink and cooked through, about 3-4 minutes on each side.

- Remove the skillet from the heat and add the butter, lemon juice, and parsley (if using). Stir to combine.

- Serve the skillet shrimp immediately with your choice of side dishes. Enjoy!

Lentil soup

Prep time: 20 minutes

Cook time: 1 hour

Servings: 4-6

Ingredients

- 1 cup lentils, rinsed and picked through

- 2 cloves garlic, minced

- 1 small onion, diced

- 2 carrots, diced

- 1 celery stalk, diced

- 1 small potato, peeled and diced

- 1 can diced tomatoes

- 4 cups chicken or vegetable broth

- 1 bay leaf

- 1 tsp thyme

- 1 tsp paprika

- 1 tsp cumin

- 1/2 tsp salt

- 1/4 tsp black pepper

Directions

- In a large pot, heat 1 tbsp olive oil over medium heat. Add the garlic, onion, carrots, and celery and cook for 5-7 minutes until the vegetables are soft.

- Add the lentils, potato, diced tomatoes, broth, bay leaf, thyme, paprika, cumin, salt, and black pepper to the pot. Bring the mixture to a boil, then reduce the heat to low and simmer for 45-60 minutes until the lentils are tender.

- Remove the bay leaf and use an immersion blender to blend the soup until it reaches your desired consistency.

- Serve the soup hot, garnished with chopped fresh herbs if desired. Enjoy!

Chicken meatballs

Prep time: 20 minutes

Cook time: 15-20 minutes

Servings: 4-6

Ingredients

- 1 pound ground chicken

- 1 egg, beaten

- 1/4 cup breadcrumbs

- 1/4 cup grated Parmesan cheese

- 1 tablespoon Italian seasoning

- 1/2 teaspoon salt

- 1/4 teaspoon black pepper

- 1 clove garlic, minced

- 1 tablespoon olive oil

Directions

- In a large bowl, mix together the ground chicken, egg, breadcrumbs, Parmesan cheese, Italian seasoning, salt, pepper, and garlic until well combined.

- Shape the mixture into small meatballs, about 1-inch in diameter.

- Heat the olive oil in a large skillet over medium heat.

- Add the meatballs to the skillet and cook for 15-20 minutes, or until they are cooked through and browned on all sides.

- Serve the meatballs with your favorite sauce or dipping sauce and enjoy!

Saffron rice

Prep Time: 10 minutes

Cook Time: 20 minutes

Servings: 4

Ingredients

- 1 cup uncooked basmati rice

- 2 cups water

- 1 pinch saffron threads

- 2 tablespoons butter or oil

- Salt to taste

Directions

- Rinse the rice in a fine mesh sieve and set aside.

- In a medium saucepan, bring the water to a boil. Add the saffron threads and stir to dissolve.

- Add the rice to the saucepan and stir to combine. Reduce the heat to low and cover the saucepan with a lid.

- Cook the rice for about 20 minutes, or until the water has been absorbed and the rice is tender.

- Remove the saucepan from the heat and add the butter or oil. Stir to coat the rice evenly.

- Season with salt to taste and serve hot. Enjoy!

Rice with tomato and tuna

Prep Time: 10 minutes

Cook Time: 20 minutes

Servings: 2

Ingredients

- 1 cup uncooked white rice

- 1 cup diced tomatoes

- 1 can tuna, drained and flaked

- 1 tablespoon olive oil

- 1 teaspoon garlic powder

- 1 teaspoon Italian seasoning

- Salt and pepper to taste

Directions

- Rinse the rice in a fine mesh strainer under cold running water.

- In a medium saucepan, bring 2 cups of water to a boil. Add the rice and stir. Reduce the heat to a simmer and cover the pot.

- Cook the rice for 18-20 minutes, or until the water has been absorbed and the rice is tender.

- While the rice is cooking, heat the olive oil in a large skillet over medium heat. Add the diced tomatoes and cook for 2-3 minutes, until they start to soften.

- Add the tuna to the skillet and stir to combine with the tomatoes. Sprinkle with garlic powder, Italian seasoning, salt, and pepper.

- Once the rice is finished cooking, add it to the skillet with the tomato and tuna mixture. Stir to combine and cook for an additional 2-3 minutes, until everything is heated through.

- Serve hot and enjoy!

Farro with steamed mussels

Prep Time: 15 minutes

Cook Time: 20 minutes

Servings: 4

Ingredients

- 1 cup farro

- 2 cups water

- 1 pound mussels, cleaned and debearded

- 1 tablespoon olive oil

- 1 small onion, finely chopped

- 2 cloves garlic, minced

- 1 cup white wine

- 1 tablespoon butter

- Salt and pepper, to taste

Directions

- Rinse the farro in a fine mesh sieve. In a medium saucepan, bring the water to a boil. Add the farro and reduce the heat to a simmer. Cook for 15-20 minutes, or until the farro is tender.

- While the farro is cooking, heat the olive oil in a large saucepan over medium heat. Add the onion and garlic and sauté until the onion is translucent, about 5 minutes.

- Add the mussels and white wine to the saucepan. Cover and cook for 5-7 minutes, or until the mussels have opened. Discard any mussels that do not open.

- Drain the farro and add it to the saucepan with the mussels. Stir in the butter and season with salt and pepper. Serve hot.

Quinoa salad

Prep time: 10 minutes

Cook time: 15 minutes

Servings: 4

Ingredients

- 1 cup quinoa

- 1 cup water

- 1 cup cherry tomatoes, halved

- 1 cup cucumber, diced

- 1 cup red bell pepper, diced

- 1 cup cooked and diced chicken

- 1/4 cup diced red onion

- 1/4 cup feta cheese

- 1/4 cup chopped fresh basil

- 1/4 cup olive oil

- 1 tablespoon red wine vinegar

- 1 clove garlic, minced

- Salt and pepper to taste

Directions

- Rinse quinoa in a fine mesh strainer.

- In a medium saucepan, bring quinoa and water to a boil. Reduce heat to low and simmer, covered, for 15 minutes or until quinoa is tender and water is absorbed.

- Remove from heat and fluff with a fork. Set aside to cool.

- In a large bowl, combine cooled quinoa, cherry tomatoes, cucumber, bell pepper, chicken, red onion, feta cheese, and basil.

- In a small bowl, whisk together olive oil, red wine vinegar, garlic, salt, and pepper.

- Pour dressing over quinoa mixture and toss to coat.

- Serve chilled or at room temperature. Enjoy!

Parsley salmon bake

Prep time: 15 minutes

Cook time: 20 minutes

Servings: 4

Ingredients

- 4 salmon fillets

- 1 cup parsley, finely chopped

- 1/2 cup breadcrumbs

- 1/4 cup parmesan cheese, grated

- 1/4 cup olive oil

- 1 lemon, zested and juiced

- 1/2 tsp salt

- 1/4 tsp black pepper

Directions:

- Preheat the oven to 400 degrees F.

- In a small bowl, mix together the parsley, breadcrumbs, parmesan cheese, olive oil, lemon zest, lemon juice, salt, and pepper.

- Place the salmon fillets on a baking sheet lined with parchment paper.

- Top each fillet with the parsley mixture, pressing down gently to ensure it sticks to the fish.

- Bake for 20 minutes, or until the salmon is cooked through and the topping is golden and crispy.

- Serve the parsley salmon bake with your choice of sides and enjoy!

Popcorn

Prep time: 5 minutes

Cook time: 5 minutes

Servings: 4

Ingredients

- 1/2 cup popcorn kernels

- 2 tbsp cooking oil

- Salt (optional)

Directions

- In a medium-sized pot, heat the cooking oil over medium heat.

- Add the popcorn kernels and cover the pot with a lid.

- Shake the pot gently to evenly distribute the kernels in the oil.

- As the kernels start to pop, continue shaking the pot to prevent burning.

- Once the popping slows down, remove the pot from the heat and let it sit for a minute to allow any remaining kernels to pop.

- Remove the lid and sprinkle with salt if desired.

- Serve immediately and enjoy!

Roasted branzino with potatoes

Prep Time: 10 minutes

Cook Time: 20 minutes

Servings: 2

Ingredients

- 2 branzino fillets

- 1 pound small potatoes, quartered

- 1 lemon, thinly sliced

- 2 tablespoons olive oil

- Salt and pepper to taste

- Fresh herbs for garnish (optional)

Directions

- Preheat your oven to 400°F.

- Place the potatoes on a large baking sheet and toss with 1 tablespoon of olive oil and a pinch of salt and pepper. Roast in the oven for 10 minutes.

- While the potatoes are roasting, prepare the branzino. Pat the fillets dry and season with salt and pepper.

- After the potatoes have roasted for 10 minutes, remove the baking sheet from the oven and push the potatoes to the edges to create space in the middle. Place the branzino fillets in the middle of the baking sheet and top each fillet with lemon slices.

- Drizzle the remaining tablespoon of olive oil over the branzino and potatoes.

- Return the baking sheet to the oven and continue roasting for another 10 minutes, or until the branzino is cooked through and the potatoes are tender.

- Garnish with fresh herbs, if desired, and serve immediately.

Shrimps with carrots

Prep time: 10 minutes

Cook time: 10 minutes

Servings: 4

Ingredients

- 1 pound shrimp, peeled and deveined

- 2 cups carrots, sliced

- 1 tablespoon olive oil

- 1 clove garlic, minced

- Salt and pepper to taste

Directions

- In a large pan, heat the olive oil over medium heat.

- Add the minced garlic and cook for 1-2 minutes until fragrant.

- Add the sliced carrots and cook for 5-6 minutes until they are tender.

- Add the shrimp to the pan and cook for an additional 3-4 minutes until they are pink and cooked through.

- Season with salt and pepper to taste.

- Serve hot and enjoy!

Lemon salmon with green beans

Prep time: 10 minutes

Cook time: 15 minutes

Servings: 4

Ingredients

- 1 lb salmon fillets

- 1 lemon, zested and juiced

- 1 tbsp olive oil

- 1/4 tsp salt

- 1/4 tsp pepper

- 1 lb green beans, trimmed

- 1 tbsp butter

Directions

- Preheat your oven to 400°F.

- Place the salmon fillets in a baking dish and season with the lemon zest, lemon juice, olive oil, salt, and pepper.

- Bake the salmon for 10-12 minutes or until it is cooked to your desired level of doneness.

- While the salmon is cooking, bring a pot of salted water to a boil. Add the green beans and cook for 2-3 minutes or until they are tender.

- Drain the green beans and transfer them to a pan with the butter. Stir to coat the green beans in the butter.

- Serve the salmon with the green beans on the side. Enjoy!

Minestrone

Prep time: 20 minutes

Cook time: 1 hour

Servings: 6

Ingredients

- 1 tablespoon olive oil

- 1 medium onion, diced

- 2 cloves garlic, minced

- 1 medium carrot, diced

- 1 celery stalk, diced

- 1 medium zucchini, diced

- 1 cup green beans, trimmed and cut into 1-inch pieces

- 2 cups vegetable broth

- 1 can diced tomatoes

- 1 can kidney beans, drained and rinsed

- 1 cup small pasta, such as ditalini or elbow

- 2 cups baby spinach

- 1/4 cup chopped fresh parsley

- Salt and pepper to taste

Directions

- Heat the olive oil in a large pot over medium heat. Add the onion, garlic, carrot, and celery and cook until the vegetables are softened, about 5 minutes.

- Add the zucchini and green beans to the pot and cook for an additional 2 minutes.

- Pour in the vegetable broth, diced tomatoes, and kidney beans. Bring the mixture to a boil, then reduce the heat to a simmer.

- Add the pasta to the pot and cook until tender, about 10 minutes.

- Stir in the spinach and parsley and cook for an additional 2 minutes.

- Season the minestrone with salt and pepper to taste. Serve hot.

Linguine with creamy mush-room sauce

Prep Time: 10 minutes

Cook Time: 20 minutes

Servings: 4

Ingredients

- 8 ounces (226 grams, 0,5 pound) linguine

- 1 tablespoon olive oil

- 8 ounces (226 grams, 0,5 pound) mushrooms, sliced

- 2 cloves garlic, minced

- 1/4 cup white wine

- 1 cup heavy cream

- 1/4 cup grated Parmesan cheese

- salt and pepper to taste

- chopped fresh parsley for garnish

Directions

- Bring a large pot of salted water to a boil. Add the linguine and cook according to package instructions until al dente.

- In a large skillet, heat the olive oil over medium heat. Add the mushrooms and cook until they are tender, about 5 minutes.

- Add the garlic and cook for an additional minute.

- Pour in the white wine and let it cook down for a few minutes.

- Add the heavy cream and bring the mixture to a simmer.

- Stir in the Parmesan cheese until it is melted and the sauce is thickened. Season with salt and pepper to taste.

- Drain the linguine and add it to the skillet with the mushroom sauce. Toss to coat the linguine evenly.

- Serve the linguine hot, garnished with chopped parsley.

Chicken souvlaki with baked zucchini

Prep Time: 15 minutes

Cook Time: 20 minutes

Servings: 4

Ingredients

- 1 pound boneless, skinless chicken breasts, cut into 1-inch pieces

- 1 medium zucchini, sliced into 1/4-inch rounds

- 1/2 cup olive oil

- 1/4 cup lemon juice

- 3 cloves garlic, minced

- 1 teaspoon dried oregano

- 1 teaspoon dried thyme

- Salt and pepper, to taste

Directions

- Preheat the oven to 400°F.

- In a small bowl, mix together the olive oil, lemon juice, garlic, oregano, thyme, salt, and pepper.

- Place the chicken pieces in a large bowl and pour the marinade over them. Toss to coat the chicken evenly.

- Thread the chicken onto skewers and place them on a baking sheet.

- Place the zucchini slices on the same baking sheet, drizzle with a little bit of olive oil, and sprinkle with salt and pepper.

- Bake for 20 minutes, or until the chicken is cooked through and the zucchini is tender.

- Serve the chicken souvlaki with the baked zucchini on the side. Enjoy!

Baked fish with basil served with a quinoa salad

Prep time: 15 minutes

Cook time: 20 minutes

Servings: 4

Ingredients

- 4 fish fillets

- 1/4 cup olive oil

- 1/4 cup lemon juice

- 1/4 cup fresh basil, chopped

- Salt and pepper to taste

- 1 cup quinoa

- 2 cups water

- 1/2 cup cherry tomatoes, halved

- 1/2 cup cucumber, diced

- 1/4 cup red onion, diced

- 1/4 cup feta cheese, crumbled

- 2 tbsp red wine vinegar

- 2 tbsp olive oil

Directions

- Preheat your oven to 400°F.

- In a small bowl, mix together the olive oil, lemon juice, and chopped basil.

- Place the fish fillets in a baking dish and season with salt and pepper. Pour the basil mixture over the fish and bake for 20 minutes, or until the fish is cooked through.

- Meanwhile, rinse the quinoa in a fine mesh sieve and place in a saucepan with 2 cups of water. Bring to a boil, then reduce the heat to low and simmer for 15 minutes, or until the quinoa is tender.

- In a large bowl, mix together the cherry tomatoes, cucumber, red onion, feta cheese, red wine vinegar, and olive oil.

- Once the quinoa is cooked, fluff it with a fork and add it to the bowl with the vegetables. Toss to combine.

- Serve the baked fish with the quinoa salad on the side. Enjoy!

Mediterranean shrimp served over whole-wheat pasta

Prep Time: 20 minutes

Cook Time: 15 minutes

Servings: 4

Ingredients

- 1 pound whole-wheat pasta

- 1 pound large shrimp, peeled and deveined

- 1 tablespoon olive oil

- 2 cloves garlic, minced

- 1 cup cherry tomatoes, halved

- 1/2 cup diced bell pepper

- 1/2 cup pitted olives, halved

- 1/4 cup white wine

- 1/4 cup chopped fresh parsley

- Salt and pepper to taste

Directions

- Bring a large pot of salted water to a boil. Add the pasta and cook according to package instructions.

- In a large skillet, heat the olive oil over medium heat. Add the garlic and cook for 1 minute until fragrant.

- Add the shrimp to the skillet and cook for 2-3 minutes on each side until pink and cooked through.

- Add the cherry tomatoes, bell pepper, and olives to the skillet and cook for an additional 2-3 minutes until the vegetables are tender.

- Pour in the white wine and bring to a simmer. Cook for 1-2 minutes until the alcohol has cooked off.

- Drain the pasta and add it to the skillet with the shrimp and vegetables. Toss to combine.

- Serve the pasta and shrimp mixture topped with chopped parsley and seasoned with salt and pepper to taste.

Roasted vegetable chickpea bowls

Prep time: 15 minutes

Cook time: 40 minutes

Servings: 4

Ingredients

- 1 cup diced carrots

- 1 cup diced zucchini

- 1 cup diced bell peppers

- 1 cup diced onions

- 1 cup diced eggplant

- 1 can chickpeas, drained and rinsed

- 2 tbsp olive oil

- 2 tsp garlic powder

- 2 tsp paprika

- 2 tsp cumin

- Salt and pepper to taste

- 4 cups cooked rice or quinoa

- Fresh herbs for garnish (optional)

Directions

- Preheat your oven to 400°F (200°C).

- On a large baking sheet, combine the diced carrots, zucchini, bell peppers, onions, and eggplant.

- Add the chickpeas to the baking sheet.

- Drizzle the vegetables and chickpeas with olive oil and sprinkle with the garlic powder, paprika, cumin, salt, and pepper.

- Toss everything together to evenly coat the vegetables and chickpeas with the spices.

- Roast the vegetables and chickpeas in the preheated oven for 40 minutes, or until the vegetables are tender and slightly caramelized.

- Divide the cooked rice or quinoa among four bowls.

- Top each bowl with the roasted vegetables and chickpeas.

- Garnish with fresh herbs, if desired.

Side Dishes

Corn Sticks

Cook time: 20 mins

Servings: 7

Ingredients

- 2 teaspoons unsalted butter melted

- 1 tablespoon plus 1 teaspoon mild vegetable oil

- 2 tablespoons unbleached all-purpose flour

- 3/4 cup fine-grind stone-ground yellow cornmeal

- 1 tablespoon granulated sugar

- 1/2 teaspoon baking powder

- 1/2 teaspoon baking soda

- 1/4 teaspoon kosher salt

- 1/2 cup buttermilk (either low-fat or full-fat)

- 1 large egg lightly beaten

Directions

- To prepare the corn sticks, position the oven rack in the center position and preheat the oven to 425°F (218°C).

- In a small saucepan over low heat, melt the butter with 1 teaspoon of the oil. Use a pastry brush to coat each corn stick pan well generously with the butter-oil mixture. Place the corn stick pan in the oven to heat while you mix the batter.

- In a large bowl, stir together the flour, cornmeal, sugar, baking powder, baking soda, and salt. Add the buttermilk, egg, and the remaining 1 tablespoon oil and use a large spoon to stir the batter slowly, just until the ingredients are combined. There will be some small lumps; that's okay. No need to panic.

- Remove the corn stick pan from the oven and spoon about 2 tablespoons of the batter into each well. The batter should fill the well to the rim.

- Bake the corn sticks until the tops are lightly browned and a toothpick inserted in the center comes out clean, about 15 minutes. If you peek at the bottom of the corn sticks, they'll be browned. Let the corn sticks cool in the pan on a wire rack for 5 minutes (but no longer than that).

- Use a small, sharp knife and your fingers to loosen the edges of the corn sticks and carefully move the sticks from the pan to the rack. Don't turn the pan upside down to release the corn sticks because their weight may break them. Serve warm.

- Use a small, sharp knife and your fingers to loosen the edges of the corn sticks and carefully move the sticks from the pan to the rack. Don't turn the pan upside down to release the corn sticks because their weight may break them. Serve warm.

Seafood stew

Prep time: 5 mins

Cook time: 25 mins

Servings: 4

Ingredients

- 1 tbsp olive oil

- 1 large onion, finely sliced

- 1 garlic clove, finely chopped

- 1 ½ tsp smoked paprika

- 400g tin chopped tomatoes

- 600ml chicken stock

- 450g (14 1/2oz) skinless white fish fillets, such as cod or haddock, chopped into large chunks

- 175g (6oz) raw peeled king prawns

- 200g (7oz) mussels, cleaned and debearded (discard any that don't close when firmly tapped)

- small bunch flat-leaf parsley, leaves roughly chopped

- crusty bread and butter, to serve (optional)

Directions

- Heat the oil in a heavy-based pan with a lid. Add the onion and cook for 5 mins, or until softened. Stir in the garlic and paprika, cook for 2 mins, then pour in the tomatoes and stock; season. Bring to the boil, then reduce to a simmer for 10 mins.

- Add the fish chunks and continue cooking for 2 mins. Add the prawns and mussels, then cover and cook for 3 mins. Discard any mussels that haven't opened, then scatter over the parsley.

- Spoon into shallow bowls and serve with crusty bread and butter, if you like.

Zucchini puree

Prep time: 10 min

Cook time: 12 min

Servings: 6

Ingredients

- 4 large Zucchini

Directions

- Wash, peel and cut zucchini into 3-inch cylindrical chunks, so that you can puree or reserve them as finger foods.

- Place in a steamer insert or a double broiler.

- Steam between 10 to 12 minutes. Zucchinis are done when they can be pierced with a fork.

- Set aside a few slices to offer as finger foods if desired.

- Transfer the rest to a blender and puree.

Swiss chard gratin

Prep: 15 mins

Cook: 40 mins

Servings: 4

Ingredients

- 400g Swiss chard

- 3 star anise

- 200g golden caster sugar

- 300g white wine vinegar

- 1 tbsp coriander seeds

- 1 tbsp white pepper

- 1 tbsp fennel seeds

- 300ml pot double cream

- 3 garlic cloves, grated

- 100g gruyère, grated

- good pinch of cayenne pepper

Directions

- To pickle the chard, put 400ml water in a large saucepan or sauté pan with the star anise, sugar and vinegar. Put the remaining spices in a cloth bag tied with string, add to the pan, bring to the boil, then drop in the chard, stalk first. Press the chard down in the pan and simmer for 3-4 mins – don't worry if you can't cover the leaves completely in the liquid, as they will wilt and become submerged while cooking. Remove the pan from the heat and leave to cool.

- Heat oven to 180C/160C fan/gas 4. Once cooled, remove the chard from the pickle mix and pat dry with a clean kitchen towel. Lay the chard in an A4-sized baking dish. In a bowl, whisk the cream and garlic together with some seasoning, then pour over the chard. Sprinkle over the cheese and cayenne pepper, and bake for 30 mins.

Pumpkin patties

Cook time: 20 mins

Servings: 4

Ingredients

- Frying oil

- 1 pound fresh peeled pumpkin

- ½ cup all purpose flour

- 1 egg beaten

- 1 teaspoon vanilla extract

- ½ teaspoon cinnamon

- ¼ teaspoon ground cloves

- 4 tablespoons sugar

- ¼ teaspoon salt

Directions

- After cooking the pumkin in boiling water with salt to taste, let it drain for about 30 minutes to remove as much water as possible.

- In a large bowl, combine the flour, salt, cinnamon, cloves and sugar.

- Then add the pumpkin, egg and vanilla.

- Mix until you have created a thick mass.

- Adjust the consistency of the mixture with flour if necessary.

- Test the taste and add more sugar if necessary.

- Heat oil to 375 degrees F.

- Take a spoonful of mixture and fry until golden brown on both sides.

- Drain on absorbent paper.

- They should be tender

Spicy sesame broccoli

Prep time: 10 mins

Cook time: 20 mins

Servings: 6

Ingredients

- 4 broccoli crowns

- 2 ½ tablespoons canola oil

- 2 tablespoons Chinese chile-garlic sauce or Sambal Oelek

- 2 teaspoons toasted sesame oil

- 2 teaspoons raw sugar or light brown sugar

- 2-3 cloves garlic peeled and minced

- salt to taste

Directions

- Preheat oven to 425°F. Lightly spray a large, rimmed baking sheet with non-stick cooking spray (or use a stoneware pan without spray.) Set aside.

- In a large mixing bowl, stir together the canola oil, chile-garlic sauce, sesame oil, raw sugar and minced garlic until even.

- Slice the broccoli crowns into long spears, keeping as much of the stem area intact as possible. Do not cut the spears too small or they'll burn instead of cooking to the desired crisp tender stage. Add all of the broccoli spears to the mixing bowl with the oil mixture and toss until everything is evenly coated. Transfer to the prepared pan, arranging the spears so they are in a single layer and sprinkle with salt to taste.

- Bake for 20-25 minutes, or until there are darkened, black, wilted edges on the cut areas and florets of the broccoli. Remove from the oven and serve immediately with hot, cooked rice or as an accompaniment to a stir fried meats or tofu.

Mash avocado chicken salad

Prep Time: 10 mins

Cook Time: 15 mins

Servings: 6

Ingredients

- 2 pieces boneless skinless chicken breasts

- 2 large avocados

- 2 tablespoons | 30 ml lemon juice

- 1/2 cup celery, finely chopped

- 1/2 cup green onions, thinly sliced

- 1/4 cup | 28 grams slivered almonds

- 1/2 teaspoon salt

- 1/2 teaspoon black pepper + more to taste

- 1/2 cup fresh cilantro or parsley, stems removed & chopped

Directions

Chicken Prep

- Lay the chicken breasts at the bottom of a medium sized sauce pan - make sure not to overlap the chicken so they cook evenly. Cover with at least 2 inches of cold water. Add the salt. Bring the chicken to a boil over a medium/heat and then cover and reduce down to a simmer. Let gently simmer for about 15 minutes to cook internally.

- Once done remove the chicken from the water and let cool a couple of minutes. You should be able to easily shred the chicken with a couple of forks at this point.

- Add the avocados and lemon juice to a large salad bowl. Mash with a fork until little to no lumps remain.

- Stir in the celery, spring onions and herbs along with the shredded chicken breasts. Taste and season with more salt and pepper as needed and enjoy!

- Serve as is, in lettuce wraps or as a sandwich.

Avocado quinoa salad with herbs

Prep Time: 5 minutes

Cook Time: 30 minutes

Servings: 2 servings

Ingredients

- 1 cup quinoa

- 2 cups vegetable stock

- 1 cup kale chopped

- 1/4 cup fresh parsley chopped

- 1/4 cup cilantro chopped

- 2 scallions thinly sliced

- zest of 1 lime

- juice of 1 lime

- 1/4 cup avocado oil or olive oil if you prefer

- 1 tsp salt

- 1/4 tsp cayenne

- 1/4 tsp red pepper flakes

- 1 avocado diced

- 1/4 cup sunflower seeds

Directions

- Prepare the quinoa (using vegetable stock in place of water), according to the package instructions.

- Set aside to cool slightly

- In a large bowl, combine kale, parsley, cilantro, scallions and cooked quinoa

- In a small bowl, combine lime zest, lime juice, salt, pepper, cayenne, and red pepper flakes.

- Slowly drizzle in avocado oil and stir to combine dressing.

- Pour dressing over salad and mix well.

- Place in refrigerator for 30 min - 1 hour to allow flavors to marinade

- Remove from fridge and garnish with sunflower seeds and diced avocado.

- Enjoy!

Desserts

Poached pears

Prep time: 15 min

Cook time: 30 min

Servings: 4

Ingredients

- 1 1/2 cups (375 ml) water

- 1 1/2 cups (375 ml) sugar

- 1 tablespoon (15 ml) lemon juice

- 4 ripe but firm pears

Directions

- In a small saucepan, bring the water, sugar, and lemon juice to a boil. Simmer for 2 to 3 minutes.

- Peel the pears, being careful to keep the stalk. With a melon baller, core the pears from the base up, so as to keep the pears whole.

- Place the pears upright in the simmering syrup and cook for about 20 minutes over low heat, according to the firmness of the pears, until tender with a knife. Remove from the heat, let cool, then refrigerate the pears in the syrup until completely chilled. Remove the pears and reduce the syrup until syrupy. Refrigerate or serve warm.

Roast plums with yoghurt and granola

Prep time: 15 mins

Total time: 1 hr

Servings: 6

Ingredients

- 6 plums, pitted and each cut into 6 wedges

- ¼ cup fresh orange juice

- 3 tablespoons light brown sugar

- 1 ½ tablespoons butter, melted

- ⅛ teaspoon salt

- 2 cups vanilla 2% reduced-fat Greek yogurt

- 2 cups low-fat granola (without raisins)

- 1 ½ tablespoons chopped pistachios

Directions

- Preheat oven to 400°.

- Combine plums, juice, sugar, butter, and salt in a bowl, tossing gently to coat. Transfer plums to a 13 x 9-inch broiler-safe baking dish. Bake at 400° for 20 minutes or until plums are very soft.

- Turn oven to broil (leave dish in oven). Broil plums 4 minutes or until pan juices are syrupy. Remove from oven; cool completely.

•Place 2 plum wedges in the bottom of each of 6 parfait glasses. Layer with about 2 1/2 tablespoons yogurt and about 2 1/2 tablespoons granola. Repeat layers once. Top each parfait with 2 more plum wedges, and drizzle each with 1 1/2 tablespoons pan juices. Sprinkle evenly with pistachios.

Watermelon wedges with feta and mint

Prep Time: 15 minutes

Servings: 6

Ingredients

- 12 wedges watermelon, about 1-inch thick

- 2 ounces (0,12 pound, 56 grams) feta cheese, crumbled

- 2 tablespoons fresh mint leaves, torn

- 1 tablespoon chile-lime powder, such as Tajin

Directions

- Lay out the watermelon wedges on a large platter. Sprinkle the feta, mint and chile-lime powder over the watermelon. Serve.

Apple tart

Prep Time: 20 mins

Total Time: 1 hr 30 mins

Servings: 8

Ingredients

For the filling

- 5 apples, peeled, cored, and sliced

- 1/3 c. packed brown sugar Juice of 1/2 lemon

- 1 tsp. ground cinnamon

- 1 tsp. pure vanilla extract

For the crust

- 1 1/3 c. all-purpose flour

- 1/4 c. packed brown sugar

- 1/2 tsp. kosher salt

- 1/4 tsp. ground cinnamon

- 10 tbsp. butter, melted

- 1 tbsp. granulated sugar

- 2 tbsp. butter, cut into small cubes

- Melted apricot preserves

Directions

- Preheat oven to 350°. In a large bowl, toss apples, brown sugar, lemon juice, cinnamon, vanilla, and salt together.

- In a large bowl, whisk together flour, sugar, salt, and cinnamon. Add melted butter and stir until dough forms. Press mixture into a 10" or 11" tart pan with a removable bottom, pressing until dough is smooth. Arrange apples over crust, sprinkle with granulated sugar and dot top with butter. Bake until crust is golden and apples are tender, about 1 hour.

- Brush with melted apricot preserves and let cool slightly before slicing and serving.

Berries and Meringue

Prep time: 8 mins

Servings: 2

Ingredients

- 2 large scoops of vanilla ice cream

- 200 g blueberries

- 2 shop-bought meringues

- 100 g raspberries

- Dark chocolate , (70%), to serve

Directions

- Get your ice cream out of the freezer.

- Put the blueberries into a non-stick frying pan with a splash of water and place on a high heat for 2 minutes, or until they all start to burst and get jammy, then remove from the heat.

- Layering up as you like, crumble the meringues between glasses or bowls, halve and add the raspberries and a nice round scoop of ice cream to each, then spoon over the jammy blueberries and their juices.

- Shave or grate over a little chocolate and tuck in, rippling it all together in a wonderful collision of flavours.

Café frappè

Prep time: 5 min

Servings: 1

Ingredients

- 3 medium scoops vanilla ice cream

- 1 cup ice

- 1 cup chilled brewed coffee

- 1/2 cup milk

- 2 tablespoons Simple Syrup for Iced Coffee Drinks

- Whipped cream

- Cocoa powder

Directions

- Blend ice cream, ice, coffee, milk, and simple syrup in a blender until smooth. Pour into a tall glass. Top with whipped cream, and dust with cocoa powder.

Pear croustade

Prep time: 1hr

Ingredients

- 1 cup all-purpose flour

- 1 ½ tablespoons sugar

- ⅛ teaspoon salt

- 6 tablespoons chilled unsalted butter, cut into 1/2 inch pieces

- 1 large egg yolk

- 1 1/2 tablespoons ice water

- 2 firm but ripe bosc pears, peeled, quartered, cored, cut into 1/2 inch wedges

- 3 tablespoons sugar

- 1 tablespoon fresh lemon juice

- 1/4 teaspoon ground allspice

- 1 large egg white, beaten to blend

- 1 tablespoon whipping cream

- 2 tablespoons all-purpose flour

- 1 tablespoon sugar

- 1 tablespoon chilled unsalted butter, cut into 1/2 inch piece

Directions

For Crust:

- Mix flour, sugar and salt in processor. Add butter. Using on/off turns, process until mixture resembles coarse meal. Transfer to large bowl.

- Mix egg yolk and 1 1/2 tablespoons ice water in small bowl. Using fork, blend enough yolk mixture, 1/2 tablespoon at a time, into flour mixture to form moist clumps.

- Gather dough into ball; flatten into disk. Wrap in plastic and chill until firm, about 1 hour.

- Position rack in center of oven and preheat to 400°F Roll out dough on floured parchment paper to 10-inch round.

- Transfer dough on parchment paper to large baking sheet.

Filling:

- Toss pears, sugar, flour, lemon juice and allspice in large bowl.

- Overlap pear slices atop dough, leaving 2-inch border. Fold border over fruit, pleating loosely and pinching to seal any cracks.

- Brush dough with egg white and drizzle cream over filing.

Topping:

- Mix flour and sugar in small bowl. Rub in butter with fingertips until mixture forms small clumps and sprinkle topping over filling.

- Bake tart until crust is golden and filling bubbles about 40 minutes.

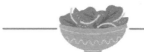

Apple croustade

Prep time: 2 hours

Servings: 4

Ingredients

Croustade dough

- 2 eggs, separated

- 2 pinches of sea salt

- 1 tsp caster sugar

- 260ml of warm water, at about 50°C

- 500g of strong white bread flour, ideally organic and from Shipton Mill

- 3g of fresh yeast, crumbled

- 2 tbsp of grapeseed oil

To finish the dough

- 15g of clarified butter

- 30g of caster sugar

Apple rosace

- 30g of clarified butter

- 1/2 tsp Calvados, or brandy

- 10g of caster sugar

- 1/4 lemon, juiced

- 8 Cox's Orange Pippin apples

Apple coulis

- 80g of Cox's Orange Pippin apple, peeled and chopped

- 80ml of water

- 40g of caster sugar

- 10ml of lemon juice

- 1/2 tsp vanilla syrup

To serve

- 8g of crystallised stem ginger, chopped (optional)

- ice cream, or sorbet, in your flavour of choice

Directions

- Make the croustade dough by whisking the egg whites with the salt and sugar until foamy. In a separate bowl, whisk the egg yolks with 240ml of the warm water, then stir this into the egg whites. Place the flour and yeast into the bowl of a stand mixer with a dough hook attachment, then run on a low speed and slowly incorporate the egg mixture

2 eggs, separated

2 pinches of sea salt

1 tsp caster sugar

240ml of warm water, at about 50°C

500g of strong white bread flour, ideally organic and from Shipton Mill

3g of fresh yeast, crumbled

- When the dough starts to come away from the sides of the bowl, add a third of the oil and continue mixing until absorbed. Add the remaining 20ml of water and continue to mix on a low speed for 10 minutes. Add the remaining oil and mix for 4 more minutes on a medium speed until absorbed, then turn the dough out onto a lightly floured surface and knead by hand into a smooth ball. Divide into 4, wrap each in cling film and refrigerate overnight

2 tbsp of grapeseed oil

20ml of warm water, at about 50°C

- The next day, place 3 of the balls of dough into the freezer for future use. Leave the remaining ball of dough out at room temperature for 4 hours before shaping

- To shape the croustades, it helps if you have someone else to assist you. Cover your work surface with a large, clean cloth, then gradually pull and stretch the dough on the cloth with someone else on the other side. Using the minimum of flour and the back of your hands, continue to stretch the dough until it is very thin. Use a pastry brush to apply a thin coat of clarified butter over the dough, then sprinkle with caster sugar

15g of clarified butter

30g of caster sugar

Snack

Healthy Almond biscotti

Yields: 18 biscotti

Ingredients

- 1 ¼ cups (150g) white whole wheat flour or gluten-free* flour (measured like this)

- ½ tsp baking powder

- 1 large egg, room temperature

- 1 ¼ tsp almond extract

- 1 ½ tsp water

- ½ cup (96g) coconut sugar

- 2 tbsp (15g) sliced almonds (see Notes!)

Directions

- Preheat the oven to 350°F, and line a baking sheet with a silicone baking mat or parchment paper.

- In a medium bowl, whisk together the flour and baking powder. In a separate bowl, whisk together the egg, almond extract, and water. Stir in the coconut sugar. Add in the flour mixture, stirring until fully incorporated. Fold in the sliced almonds.

- Transfer the cookie dough to the prepared baking sheet, and shape into a long and skinny rectangle that's 2 ¼" wide and ¾" tall using your hands or a spatula. (If the cookie dough sticks to your hands, rub them with a little neutral-tasting oil first!)

- Bake at 350°F for 33-35 minutes. (The outside should be golden brown and very dry and crusty!) Let the rectangle of baked cookie dough cool on the baking sheet for 10 minutes (no more and no less!).

- Transfer the rectangle of baked cookie dough to a cutting board. Using a sharp serrated knife, cut the rectangle into ½"-thick strips (no wider!), working from one short end of the rectangle to the other. (Both diagonal strips and horizontal strips will work!) You should end up with cookies that are ½" thick, ¾" tall, and 2 ¼"+ wide.

- Place the cookies onto the original baking sheet with one cut side facing down and the other cut side facing up. Bake at 350°F, flipping the cookies halfway through, for 6-8 minutes (for centers with just a bit of "give") or 12-16 minutes (for centers that are completely hard and dry). Cool completely to room temperature on the baking sheet.

Sweet and savory berries

Prep time: 20 minutes

Ingredients

- Cheese (pick 3 or so):

    Soft: Brie or goat cheese

    Semi soft: Blue cheese, fontina, or havarti

    Hard: Manchego, Bellavitano, aged cheddar or gouda, Parmigiano-Reggiano

- Berries: strawberries, blueberries, raspberries and/or blackberries

- Nuts (pick 2+): walnuts, pistachios, Marcona almonds, pecans

- Dried fruit: cranberries, figs, cherries and/or raisins

- Spreads: honey, olive oil, fruit spread (such as fig jam)

- Extras: Chocolate covered nuts or fruit, dark chocolate squares, caramels

- Crackers and/or bread sticks

Directions

- Grab a big board. It can be a wooden cutting board or any serving platter.

- Arrange the cheese on the board.

- Add the sauces in little bowls.

- Arrange the berries in groups around the cheeses.

- Fill in any gaps with nuts, dried fruit, and extras.

- Add crackers or bread. Serve!

Herbed bean spread

Prep time: 20 mins

Servings: 4

Ingredients

- 1 1/2 cups cooked cannellini beans, drained and rinsed

- 1/4 cup cilantro or parsley

- 1/4 cup mixed fresh herbs, dill, tarragon, mint, and/or chives

- 2 tablespoons extra-virgin olive oil

- 3 tablespoons fresh lemon juice

- 1 tablespoon tahini

- 1 small garlic clove

- 1/2 teaspoon lemon zest

- 1/2 teaspoon sea salt, plus more to taste

- 1 to 3 tablespoons water, if needed

- Freshly ground black pepper

Directions

- In a food processor, place the cannellini beans, herbs, olive oil, lemon juice, tahini, garlic, lemon zest, salt, and several grinds of pepper. Pulse until creamy. If the mixture is too thick, add water, 1 tablespoon at a time, until it reaches a creamy consistency.

- Assemble each thin stacker with the spread, radishes, carrots, edamame, herbs, and a sprinkle of feta cheese.

Smoothie
and drinks

Warm honey green tea

Ingredients

- 4 cups water

- 4 lemon peel strips (2 1/2 x 1 inches each)

- 4 orange peel strips (2 1/2 x 1 inches each)

- 4 green tea bags

- 2 teaspoons honey

- 4 lemon slices

Directions

- Stir together the water, lemon peel strips, and orange peel strips in a medium saucepan. Bring to boiling; reduce heat. Simmer, uncovered, for 10 minutes. Remove the lemon and orange strips with a slotted spoon and discard

- Place tea bags in a teapot; immediately add the simmering water mixture. Cover and let steep according to the tea package directions (1 to 3 minutes). Remove the tea bags, squeezing gently. Discard the tea bags. Stir in honey. Pour the tea into four heatproof mugs or cups and garnish each with a lemon slice. Serve immediately.

Naturally sweetened ice green tea

Ingredients

- 1/4 cup lime juice, plus 3 limes sliced for garnish

- 1/4 cup lemon juice, plus 2 lemons sliced for garnish

- 5 cups water, (2 cups boiling, plus 3 cups cold)

- 5 tea bags, Jasmine Green Tea Bags

- 1/4 cup honey, plus more if desired (up to 1/2 cup)

- 18 mint leaves

Directions

- Transfer lime juice and lemon juice to a large pitcher.

- Bring 2 cups of water to boil in a medium saucepan. Once the water reaches 170 to 185°F, add 5 green tea bags into the hot water.

- Steep for 3 minutes or according to package instructions.

- Using a large spoon, gently press the tea bags against the pan to extract the tea further. Carefully remove and discard the tea bags from the saucepan.

- Add honey, and stir until dissolved. Pour tea and honey mixture into the pitcher.

- Add 3 cups of cold water to pitcher. Stir until well blended. Add more honey, if desired.

- Serve chilled green tea with ice cubes, a few lime slices, lemon slices and 3 fresh mint leaves in each glass.

Green tea recipe

Prep time: 2 mins

Cook time: 5 mins

Servings: 2

Ingredients

- 2 teaspoons Green tea leaves

- 2 cups Water

- Honey , (optional) to taste

Directions

- To begin making Green Tea Recipe, take a saucepan and start heating water on a high heat.

- Once the water starts boiling, turn off the heat and add the green tea leaves.

- Keep it covered for a minute.

- Strain the green tea into the tea cups.

- Add honey to taste (only as a sweetener, you can completely skip it), give it a swirl and serve.

- Serve Green tea recipe with a snack like Baked Aloo Tikki Recipe and Dhaniya Pudina Chutney Recipe (Green Chutney) during evenings.

Mediterranean smoothie

Prep Time: 5 minutes

Servings: 2

Ingredients

- 2 cups baby spinach loosely packed, organic

- 1 teaspoon ginger root fresh, minced

- 1 banana frozen, pre-sliced

- 1 mango small

- 1/2 cup beet juice beets originate in the Mediterranean

- 1/2 cup skim milk or unsweetened almond milk

- 6 ice cubes

Directions

- Toss all the above ingredients in a blender and blend until smooth.

Pineapple green smoothie

Prep Time: 2 mins

Servings: 2

Ingredients

- 1.33 cup low-fat vanilla Greek yogurt

- 2 banana

- 2 cup pineapple

- 2 cup fresh baby spinach, packed

- 0.5-1 cup apple juice, or skim milk

- Ice, optional

Directions

- Place all ingredients in a blender and puree until smooth. If using frozen fruit you'll probably need to use 1/2 cup liquid instead of just 1/4.

Very berry green smoothie

PREP TIME: 15-20 minutes

Servings: 2 servings

Ingredients

- 1 cup fresh strawberries, raspberries, blueberries or blackberries

- ½ banana

- 1 cup diced pineapple

- ½ cup chopped kale, stalks removed

- ¼ cup broccoli

- ¼ avocado, pitted and peeled

- ¾ cup orange juice

- 1 cup ice

- 2 tablespoons chia seeds

- 1 scoop (approximately 1⅓ ounces) natural or vanilla protein powder

- ⅓ cup granola, to sprinkle on top or mix into smoothie

Directions

- Combine berries, banana, pineapple, kale, broccoli, avocado, juice and ice in a blender or food processor. Pulse until smooth. Add chia seeds and protein powder, and blend until well mixed.

- Pour into glass and top with granola. (If desired, mix granola into smoothie to add a little crunch.) Serve immediately.

Cream peach smoothie

Prep Time: 1m

Servings: 1

Ingredients

- 1/2 Cup Coconut Milk (or milk of choice)

- 4-5 Slices Frozen Peach

- 2 tbsp Heavy Whipping Cream

- 2 tbsp Sweetener (Monkfruit Erythritol Blend, sugar or sweetener of choice)

Directions

1) Gather all the ingredients.

2) Place all ingredients into a blender and blend until smooth (about 10-15 seconds).

3) Pour in tall glass and enjoy!

Chocolate strawberry smoothie

Prep Time: 5 minutes

Servings: 1

Ingredients

- 1 cup frozen strawberries

- 1 banana (room temperature)

- ½ cup Old Fashioned oats (optional)

- ¼ cup cocoa powder

- 1 tablespoon almond butter

- ¾ cup milk of choice (dairy, oat milk or almond milk)

- 2 tablespoons maple syrup or honey

- 1 cup ice

- For the garnish: 1 sprinkle chopped dark chocolate (optional)

Directions

- Place all ingredients in a blender, breaking the banana into pieces. Blend until creamy and frothy, stopping and scraping down the sides as necessary and adding a splash more milk if necessary.

- If desired, top with 1 tablespoon chopped dark chocolate (it makes for a nice mix in but it's totally optional). Serve immediately or store in a covered jar in the refrigerator for 2 days.

Standard US/Metric measurement conversions

1 ounce = 28,35 grams = 0,06 pound

1 pound = 454 grams = 16 ounce

1 cup = 240 ml = 1/16 gallon = 48 teaspoons = 16 tablespoons

When it comes to cooking and baking, accurate measurement is essential for producing delicious and consistent results. However, depending on where you are in the world, you may be using different systems of measurement. In the United States, recipes typically use standard US measurement, which includes cups, tablespoons, and teaspoons. However, many other countries, including most of Europe, use the metric system, which measures volume in milliliters (mL) and weight in grams (g).

The standard measurement system used in the United States is the US system, which includes units such as inches, feet, and pounds. However, the metric system, which includes units such as meters, centimeters, and grams, is widely used around the world. It is important to be able to convert between these two systems in order to communicate effectively with others and to understand the measurements used in different parts of the world. It is important to be able to convert between these two systems in order to communicate effectively with others and to understand the measurements used in different parts of the world. **1 ounce is equal to 28.35 grams** so if you are working with a recipe that calls for ounces and you only have a metric scale, you can easily convert the measurement by multiplying the number of ounces by 28.35. For example, if a recipe calls for 4 ounces of sugar, you would need to use 113.4 grams of sugar. It's also helpful to remember that 1 pound is equal to 16 ounces and approximately 453.6 grams. By understanding these standard conversion rates, you can easily convert between the US and metric measurement systems.

For those accustomed to using standard US measurements, converting to the metric system can seem intimidating. However, with a little practice and understanding, it is a straightforward process. Here are some tips for converting standard US measurements to metric measurements in recipes:

- Understand the basic conversions. One cup is equal to approximately 237 mL, one tablespoon is equal to approximately 15 mL, and one teaspoon is equal to approximately 5 mL. These conversions will vary slightly depending on the density of the ingredient being measured, but they can be used as a general guide.

- Use a kitchen scale. A kitchen scale is a quick and easy way to measure ingredients in grams or ounces. Simply place the ingredient on the scale, reset it to zero, and add or subtract as needed.

- Use a kitchen conversion chart. There are many online resources that provide conversion charts for standard US to metric measurements. Simply find the ingredient you are using and match it to the corresponding measurement in milliliters or grams.

- Get a set of measuring cups and spoons with metric measurements. This can be a helpful tool for those who are more comfortable with standard US measurements, as it allows you to measure out ingredients using familiar tools but with metric measurements.

- Practice, practice, practice. The more you work with metric measurements, the more comfortable you will become with converting and using them in recipes. Don't be afraid to make mistakes – it's all part of the learning process.

When converting from metric to standard US measurements, the process is similar. Simply use the conversions listed above in reverse, or use a kitchen conversion chart or kitchen scale to find the corresponding standard US measurement.

It's important to note that conversions between standard US and metric measurements are not always exact. For example, 1 cup of flour may weigh slightly different in grams than 1 cup of sugar due to differences in density. In cases like these, it's best to stick with the measurement listed in the recipe, as small variations in weight or volume can have a significant impact on the final result.

In conclusion, converting between standard US and metric measurements in recipes is a simple process with a little practice and understanding. Whether you prefer to use a kitchen scale, conversion chart, or measuring cups and spoons with both systems of measurement, there are many tools and resources available to help make the process easier. With a little patience and persistence, you'll be confidently converting and using both standard US and metric measurements in your cooking and baking in no time.

28 days meal planner

	Breakfast	Lunch	Dinner
Day 1	Greek eggs	Baked cauliflower au gratin	Muffin-tin quiches with smoked cheddar & potato
Day 2	Date oats	Basil Salmon	Greek turkey burgers with spinach, feta & tzatziki
Day 3	Toast with avocado	Greek style salad	Veggie flatbread
Day 4	Yoghurt and berries	Halibut sandwiches	Lentil soup
Day 5	Artichoke and cucumber hoagies	Dijon salmon with green bean pilaf	Saffron rice
Day 6	Spinach frittata	Brussels sprouts salad with crispy chickpeas	Farro with steamed mussels
Day 7	Zucchini and ricotta egg muffins	Garlic and artichoke pasta	Parsley salmon bake
Day 8	Almond-cherry oatmeal bowls	Spaghetti with brown butter and feta	Roasted branzino with potatoes
Day 9	Easy overnight oats	Spaghetti with green bean	Lemon salmon with green beans
Day 10	Chia pudding & berries	Lemon couscous with broccoli	Linguine with creamy mushroom sauce
Day 11	Egg salad	Mediterranean lentils	Baked fish with basil served with a quinoa salad
Day 12	Italian frittata	Vegetable and tofu scramble	Roasted vegetable chickpea bowls
Day 13	Oatmeal bananas & almonds	Linguine with tapenade	Mash avocado chicken salad

Day 14	Sandwiches tomato & prosciutto	Fusilli with Italian pesto genovese	Olive caper salmon bake
Day 15	Tomato and egg scramble	Rosemary barley with walnuts	Skillet shrimp
Day 16	Basic potatoes	Eggs in tomato sauce with chickpeas & spinach	Chicken meatballs
Day 17	Zucchini and ricotta egg muffins	Greek salad with avocado	Rice with steamed mussels
Day 18	Greek yoghurt with chocolate	Chicken gyros	Parsley salmon bake
Day 19	Creamy blueberry-pecan overnight oasts	Brown rice salad with cheese	Shrimps with carrots
Day 20	Fig bowl	Mediterranean tuna-spinach salad	Minestrone
Day 21	Greek eggs	Balsamic roasted chicken and vegetables	Chicken souvlaki with baked zucchini
Day 22	Date oats	Vegetarian spaghetti squash lasagna	Mediterranean shrimp served over whole-wheat pasta
Day 23	Toast with avocado	Spaghetti with tomato and basil	Avocado quinoa salad with herbs
Day 24	Yoghurt and berries	Spaghetti with mushroom ragu	Muffin-tin quiches with smoked cheddar & potato
Day 25	Artichoke and cucumber hoagies	Penne all'arrabbiata	Veggie flatbread
Day 26	Spinach frittata	Min brown rice	Saffron rice
Day 27	Zucchini and ricotta egg muffins	Cauliflower rice with mushroom	Parsley salmon bake

| Day 28 | Greek yoghurt with chocolate | Parmesan asparagus with tomatoes | Lemon salmon with green beans |

NOTES:

Week 1
Meal Plan

Snack

Vitamins

Vegetable

Monday

Tuesady

Wednesday

Thursday

Friday

Saturday

Sunday

Week 2
Meal Plan

Snack

Vitamins

Vegetable

Monday

Tuesady

Wednesday

Thursday

Friday

Saturday

Sunday

Week 3
Meal Plan

Snack

Vitamins

Vegetable

Monday

Tuesady

Wednesday

Thursday

Friday

Saturday

Sunday

Week 4
Meal Plan

| | Monday |

Snack

| | Tuesady |

| | Wednesday |

Vitamins

| | Thursday |

| | Friday |

Vegetable

| | Saturday |

| | Sunday |

Help me grow and improve on Amazon, for me it's **very important**.

I'd love to hear your **honest opinion**,

even with photo or video of the book,

here:

https://www.abookforpress.com/reviewus/

or by scanning this code.

Thank you!

SCAN ME!

If you want, sign up for **FREE BOOKS** at "A Book For" group at Facebook

GREEN MEDITERRANEAN DIET COOKBOOK

By Cook Delicious Press

THANK YOU